MW01227511

Young Closer

A Young Entrepreneur's Guide
to Fast-Forwarding Your Success

By Zach Sasser

Bookmark
PUBLISHING HOUSE

Edited by Hilary Jastram, www.bookmarkpub.com

Dedication

This book is dedicated to all the young hustlers out there.
The ones who have big dreams but also have the work ethic and
discipline to know that they'll accomplish everything they dream of.

Keep pushing.

Get in Touch!

Facebook.com/realzachsasser

Instagram.com/sasser21

ZachSasser1.phonesites.com

Table of Contents

Foreword

As a mentor, coach, consultant, or whatever name you want to use that people have dubbed me over the years, I've written a lot of forewords for a lot of books for a lot of amazing people.

I can't say I've ever been prouder to write the foreword of a book than I am of this one.

I've watched this young man Zach Sasser go from an intern in our company to the top producing salesperson closing millions of dollars annually in our organization.

I've watched him go from being the quiet guy in the cubicle to the ultimate leader in the field.

Zach and I have traveled all over the country, attending multiple events together, making sales, friends, relationships, and tapping into new networks, so I have the privilege of knowing him better than just about anybody other than his blood family—maybe even better than some of them.

Zach embodies core values. He lives by the mission to help as many people as possible become the greatest version of themselves. He's the definition of grit.

If you see us interact online, I often refer to Zach as my son. I swear that my kids think he is their older brother; he's around in our life so much. That speaks volumes since I'm a very guarded person and don't let many people come to my house. I don't let many people know where I live, and I don't like traveling with others. My wife doesn't travel with me often, either, because what we do is all about business. But Zach's always there and always accommodating everyone else as he stays on top of his game.

I'm so proud of this young man.

This book is not your traditional rags-to-riches story. It's a book of practical, applicable knowledge and experience Zach has personally learned and used in his life. It's not metaphorical.

Within these pages is Zach's systematic approach to closing millions of dollars per year and earning millions over his career—all at only 22 years old.

If you're a young person reading this book, be inspired. Zach is showing you what's possible if you follow the blueprint he's laid out for you through the following pages.

It's a big gift for you to be here reading *Young Closer*, and it's a big achievement for Zach to have written it. Doing so separates him into the 1% zone of genius filled with people who have articulated their thoughts onto paper to make them a reality and, in Zach's case—soon to be a best seller.

Enjoy the read
Ryan Stewman

Introduction

Less than 50% of adults in the United States finished reading an entire book last year. If you are reading this book, I don't believe you to be included in this below-average majority. Don't be average.[1]

This book has been a long time coming. It feels weird saying that as a 22-year-old, but I've always made it a point to surround myself with people who push me in every aspect of my life. While most people my age are just graduating from college and getting their feet wet in a new internship or are three years deep into the hustle, I am dropping a book to help them crush the next chapter of their life.

I don't say that to brag, but you should know some points of this book may come across as bragging. Unfortunately, to some, winning and bragging sound the same. It is not my intention to brag; I say what I do to show what's possible when you're focused on the right path and surrounded by the right people.

I am beyond humbled and grateful to have lived the life I have up until this point. I am even more blessed to be saying I am just getting started.

While I never saw myself releasing a book at 22, I have decided it is selfish to get to be in the rooms I get to be in with the people I get to meet, have conversations with, learn from, pick up knowledge and wisdom, and keep it to myself.

So, I've got some things to say.

I've got some things to share.

---

[1] https://bookriot.com/american-reading-habits-2022/

> **My mission in life is to not only become the most elite version of myself but to help as many people as possible do the same.**

Part of that includes sharing what I've learned to show that while there is no shortcut to success, there is a quick path.

Start stacking a bunch of good habits on top of each other. Stay consistent and do good by people, and you will be successful.

A right path.

A proven process.

There are habits to follow and habits to avoid.

There is no magic pill or secret to success.

If you quit reading right now, I hope that lesson alone helps you. Stop looking for a secret to success and start learning the skills and habits needed to be great—the good habits you should be doing. Start living your life the right way.

In this book, I share the ten biggest secrets I believe everyone should know when getting started. I have been mentored by, learned from, and become friends with some of the country's top entrepreneurs, marketers, and businesspeople.

I've flown on private jets every other weekend with Ryan Stewman; hung with Sean Whalen in Pedregal, Cabo; Jordan Belfort and Dan Klein on Bourbon Street; and chilled with Keith Pike. Businessmen, investors, marketers, influencers, millionaires—even a couple of billionaires—are the people I'm surrounded by at all times. When you're around people of this caliber, you pick up on a thing or two.

There's a saying that you become who you surround yourself with or compare yourself to. It's 100% true. Over the past few years, I have become the person I used to dream of becoming, and I owe it all to the lessons that these remarkable people taught me—lessons that I am sharing in this book.

I want you to hear the advice given to me by Sean Whalen while we ate dinner in Cabo San Lucas, watching the most beautiful sunset I've ever seen. I want you to hear the top advice I've gotten from Ryan Stewman while spending hundreds of hours in the air with him, traveling to different speaking gigs, and logging thousands of hours simply being around him. You'll read about what the #1 RE/MAX broker in the country taught me and what guys with $4.8 billion worth of real estate under management advise me on.

I've been blessed to have these mentors, and I know the lessons and experiences from the first 22 years of my life will make me incredibly successful. I have no doubt I can turn it into a billion dollars over my lifetime. If you're younger than me and take these lessons to heart, you could turn them into more.

Even if you aren't younger than me, having these lessons at 25, 30, or 50 is better than never. It isn't about your age; it's about becoming the greatest version of yourself no matter where you are.

Everyone has different starting points, situations, goals, and obstacles. It's about becoming the best you that you can be.

If something I share in this book inspires just one person or teaches just one thing, it is worth it.

> Stay in your own lane. People start at different spots. Some people have short-term goals, and some have long-term goals. Don't compare yourself to others. Focus on you making yourself better. Compare yourself to where you were a year ago and a day ago. Don't lose that competitiveness; it's what makes you great. Learn to channel it and don't allow it to turn into hate.
> —*Lesson learned and paraphrased from Nehal Kaiser*

But before I dive into those lessons, it's important that you understand a little bit about who I am and why you should listen to what I have to say.

Chapter 1

Building the Young Closer

"Today, I will do what others won't,
so tomorrow, I can do what others can't."
–Jerry Rice

Nobody wants to read 27 pages of what six-year-old Zach did in elementary school, nor do I think anything extraordinary happened during that time, so I'll skip right to where things started to click. I went from being a normal middle-class kid to flying on private jets and creating generational wealth.

Growing up, I did well in school. I took advanced classes and got straight As. I wanted to go to Stanford to be an engineer because that's what success looked like to me at the time.

About six weeks into my eighth-grade year, things switched up. I would go to school for eight hours, then come home and sit at my kitchen table for another five hours doing homework when I realized that wasn't what I wanted to do.

Now, I had something to prove.

I've always found a way to put immense pressure on myself.

Pressure is cool and needed to make diamonds,
but if your heart isn't in it, it just creates stress.

Stress is pressure that isn't dealt with or handled.

I grew up in an entrepreneurial family. My dad owned a roofing company and was always in sales.

He never forced me into sales, but he made it a point to show me its possibilities and advantages.

I went down the rabbit hole of sales funnels, lead generation, and digital marketing. My dad and I started buying courses and immersing ourselves in the possibilities and skillsets needed to succeed in those courses and build a marketing agency.
We also made sure we were surrounded by the right people.

In eighth grade, it clicked. I saw freedom in what my dad did. The possibilities and scalability inspired me to look at marketing, sales, business and making money as a game. I discovered how wealth is accumulated. My love for problem-solving helped because that's what business is: providing value to the marketplace for a financial return.

My focus left school and my grades so I could concentrate on business. I no longer aspired to go to college or work for someone else for the rest of my life. I wanted to be a boss. I wanted to be a creator.

I also knew I wasn't here to be average. I didn't want an average life: stressing about bills, unable to take my kids on vacations and create memories with them or spend my money however I pleased.

Since you're reading this book, I assume you don't want that life, either.

In school, every time we got put into groups for projects, I was always the one carrying the weight. I solved the problems, shared new perspectives, and worked my tail end off.

I wasn't like everyone else. My work ethic was insane, and I didn't believe someone else could tell me my work was worth the same amount per hour as someone I was running circles around.

I always put forth the most effort in everything I did. Even if I wasn't the best, I was always trying to be, which directly correlates to my results.

It was time to go all in on the right path.

At 17, I was selling roofs for my dad, learning about digital marketing, and trying to piece together a way to connect them.

Eventually, I learned from a guy named Dan Klein (whom you will hear about in a later chapter) how to make websites show up first on Google through a process called Search Engine Optimization (SEO). Then I put together sites for my dad and brother. Within a year, we were #1 on Google, getting phone calls and closing $20,000 roofs—all from the skills I learned and the work I put in.

As soon as I proved my process worked, I doubled down. In my last semester of high school, I ran a full-time marketing agency while deciding whether I would go to college.

It was 50/50 on if I'd go or not.

> I still remember the first house we signed from my marketing efforts. I was 18 years old and felt like the past three years of studying sales and marketing had paid off. All the books, the nights I skipped parties to build websites, it was all worth it.

I chose to go to a local college to stay close to my family, continue my business, and get a degree just in case a worst-case scenario happened and I needed to get a job making $60k per year.

My dad was in sales when I was growing up, and we had some good years, but we also had some bad years. He said having a degree during those bad years would've helped him a little more.

I also already had almost a full year of college credits completed from courses I'd taken in high school. I received a scholarship to pay for most of my schooling, so I decided to bite the bullet and go.

I'll talk more about my formal education versus real-world experiences in Chapter 11. For now, I want to focus on the opportunity I was presented with.

My Opportunity

I moved in with my brother Brett at 18.

One day, I went to my parent's house to drop something off for my younger brothers, Kyle and Ty.

I walked into my dad's office to say hello, and he pulled me in to introduce me to someone he was on a video call with.

"This is Danny," he said. "He works with Ryan Stewman."

I'd been following Ryan for the past few years, as he was the go-to for all things sales and marketing. He was local and ran one of the biggest Facebook groups for sales professionals: Sales Talk with Sales Pros.

"Hey, what's going on, Zach? You go to the University of North Texas?"

He saw the hoodie I was wearing. "Yes sir, I do."

"Cool, man, what do you study?"

"Marketing!"

"That's what's up! Would you be interested in an internship up here with us?"

I paused for a second because I had recently realized internships were essential for getting a job after college—but I knew I didn't want a job. I wanted to be my own boss. College was a backup plan, so I didn't need an internship.

Still, I replied, "Of course." In theory, I didn't want to work for anyone, but Ryan Stewman wasn't just anyone. You don't turn down an internship with him.

I wasn't sure what I had gotten myself into at that moment and whether the casual offer would lead to anything—but after a few months and following up with Danny at least 15 times, I was at the office in Addison, Texas, as the newest intern for one of Ryan's companies, PhoneSites.

> **Lesson No. 1:**
> There are very few sales you don't close if you simply know how to follow up with people, consistently stay in front of them, and show them the value.

My first sale was closing Danny on getting me in the office as an intern.

Soon, I was making sales funnels and walking our customers through demonstrations of our software for $15 an hour, but I would've done it for free to be in the same office as Ryan.

I'm a huge believer in leading with value. I knew I'd learn a ton just from being in that room, but I was focused on being the hardest worker on the team and proving my worth.

Stewman says that if you work harder than what you're paid for, you'll eventually be paid more than you work. I took that literally and worked like a million-dollar intern.

PhoneSites is a software that generates leads to make sales. Ryan owns PhoneSites, but his main business is Apex—the step-by-step, tactical training on how to use PhoneSites and generate leads by becoming the go-to person in your industry and attracting sales to you instead of not knowing where your next sale is coming from. In addition to the training, Apex also surrounds you with one of the most elite networks out there.

Apex has been instrumental in closing millions of sales for me, easily fast-forwarding my success by ten-plus years. I'd highly recommend that you look into what Apex entails at ZachSasser1.PhoneSites.com. (Gotta show love to PhoneSites.)

I knew that every client who needed PhoneSites also needed Apex. So I made it a point to mention Apex during every demo call.

Most people who used PhoneSites knew about Apex and would ask questions about it. I'd lay the sale up right to the other sales rep at the time, and they would close it.

I went above and beyond for my clients, ensuring they had the absolute best experience with "a very impressive 20-year-old," hoping word would get to Ryan that I was doing the work. After six months, Ryan called me into his office.

"Hey man, I just want to say I appreciate your hard work. You came in as an intern, worked hard, and sent a ton of sales for our Apex program, and I appreciate that. But what do you think about us training you to sell Apex yourself?"

That was it.

I sold fewer PhoneSites and more Apex for the next couple of months. It started slow. My first five months of sales for PhoneSites as an intern were $141, $1514, $2058, $5825, $6639.

,0,0,0,0,0,0,0,0,0,0,0,0,0,0,0,0,0,0,0,0,0,0,0,0,0,0,0,0,0,0,0,0,0,0,0,0,0,0,0,0,0,0,0,0,0,0,0,0,0,0

We brought in another intern around this time, and he and I became best friends, but we also fueled each other with a healthy sense of competition. I started hitting: $13,716, $15,994, $17,714… but I was now getting paid 10% commission as opposed to 50% because Apex and PhoneSites had different commission structures. So, my income decreased for a while. But I saw the opportunity to improve at this skill set, and I wasn't going to quit until I got good.

I wasn't balling—but I was in my early twenties, so my bills weren't high. My bills still aren't high, as I believe that's a key to building wealth that I discuss more in Chapter 2. I had a small base and didn't need much for my living expenses.

I just kept doing the work that I knew would eventually pay off. I would've done it for free just to get in the room.

Next, I made the transition and started to sell Apex as my main focus: $35,908, $26,019, $27,111, $47,163.

Then in December 2020, one year after I started working with Ryan, I hit $196,569. More than 4x my highest previous month. This was the turning point for me.

We ran a special that month, and it definitely made sales easier—but Ryan told me it wasn't the deal that made me reach that amount. It was my belief in myself. That made me raise the ceiling I put on myself and realize there was no reason I couldn't hit that number every month.

My next few months were $68,161, $74,806, $143,771, $242,424, $402,674, $111,085, $287,069 for a total of $3.6 million in sales my second full year with Stewman at only 20 years old.

Despite the excuses I could've made, I kept doing the work, wanting to quit sometimes and not seeing immediate results. I now consistently hit between $400k and $600k a month, with my best month being $711k. Stewman says that puts me in the top three of the entire industry among all the sales reps selling consulting or coaching programs.

I love sales. This high-paying skill I learned to make money also allowed me to thrive in other aspects of my life, but sales isn't the focus of this book.

Money isn't everything, but it's pretty important.
Without money, you can't buy water or a place to live,
and you need that to live."
—Ryan Stewman

Money is a magnifier. If you're a good person without money, you'll be a good person with money. It's all in how you use it, and after being surrounded by so many elites, I will explain how the business elite use theirs.

Throughout my entrepreneurship journey, I've learned many valuable lessons from mentors that allowed me to avoid making the same mistakes.

> I already mentioned that success is a series of small, good habits—like working hard, doing the right thing, always learning, etc.—combined with consistency and discipline.

Many people believe there is a shortcut to success. They think things should be happening quicker for them because they are doing the work every day—but since it isn't, they must be missing a magic pill.

If you do enough of these little habits for long enough, you will become successful, but it won't happen overnight.

I may lose half of my readers by telling them I won't be giving them the magic pill to success, but for those willing to accept that, I will give you the good news.

While there is no shortcut, there is a correct path to take. Going down the wrong road can make your journey much longer. The key is establishing the right habits as quickly as possible to put you on the fast track to success.

And that's precisely my objective in this book.

To condense the condenser.

I have condensed years' worth of experiences and wisdom from the business elite and my biggest mentors into a short enough book that you could finish in one sitting if you wanted.

I'm not one for guarantees, but if you read this book and apply what you learn, I have no doubt that you will excel in every aspect of your life and get even closer to being the most elite version of yourself that God intended you to be.

Let's get to it.

Chapter 2

Little Zach: The Value of a Dollar

"The ability to discipline yourself to delay gratification in the short term in order to enjoy greater rewards in the long term is the indispensable prerequisite for success."
–Brian Tracy

When you grow up in an entrepreneurship family, you see a lot of ups and downs. I mostly saw financial downs for the first 12 years of my life. I don't want to make it sound like I was homeless or that things were worse than they were: we always had food to eat, and we always knew someone loved us, and for that, I am forever grateful. But it did mean we had free or reduced lunches.

From a young age, I learned the value of a dollar.

Even as a kid, I always knew when we were going through tough times. My parents tried to hide it the best they could, but I could read them.

The problem was that my brothers couldn't always tell. I tried my best to help my parents as much as possible. As an 8-year-old kid, the only way I knew was to save them money.

Sometimes my little brothers would ask for a toy at the store, and I would tell them we didn't need it before my mama heard them ask because I knew she hated saying no to us. I was instilled with this mindset of saving money and not buying stuff we didn't need. I was fine with eating off the dollar menu with my family and not getting the extra toys. I preferred it. Buying things stressed me out.

When I was 12, my dad started selling roofs. He's a rock star salesperson, mostly because he's super smart and genuinely wants to help people (I talk more about my dad in Chapter 4). He had some big years selling roofs—like really big years—especially for a one-rep business owner. He was doing volume that companies with 10+ employees don't do.

While my younger brothers, Kyle and Ty, saw the good years and didn't remember the tough ones, my older brother Brett and I saw the years we struggled.

Growing up poor is the biggest advantage you can have, and growing up with privilege is the biggest handicap.

There's something about seeing the bottom and knowing you don't want to be there anymore. So many celebrities—Kevin Hart, Eric Thomas, and even most of the mentors I will introduce you to in this book—come from absolutely nothing and use it to fuel their success the whole way.

The point is that I learned good money habits at a young age. Those lessons have been absolutely crucial in truly building wealth and becoming financially free.

I learned how money worked. And for that, I'm forever grateful for the years I went through the struggle. I know I could lose everything in my bank account and find a way back to the top because I learned how money works. My first mentor taught me how to be good with money.

I hate spending money.

Don't get me wrong, I spend money, but not what you'd expect a multi-million-dollar sales producer to buy.

I have no problem maxing out my IRA, investing in masterminds, events, and books, and throwing thousands at an overfunded life insurance policy every month—but I'm hesitant to buy anything that won't directly make me money.

I live well below my means for a few reasons.

1. A dollar invested is more beneficial to me than a dollar spent.

A dollar invested will work for me and bring back $1.30. That $1.30 will work for me and return $1.69. It doesn't seem like much, but when you add a few zeros to the end of those dollars, you realize why I'm so money conscious.

I don't even need that much money to live off. If you save enough money, you can invest it to earn passive income that will fund your entire life.

If I had a million dollars earning 10% each year, I could live off $100k and have a lifestyle that I enjoy. $300k invested at 30% could do the same. You don't need to invest much money to "fund your life." This example is just to show the power of investing.

2. I have big goals.

I hate to call myself "cheap." I'm not cheap; I'm just smart with my money. Luckily, I'm a simple Texas boy who doesn't care about name brands or crave materialistic items that others have. I don't need much to be satisfied. Plus, I have huge goals, and I know if I want to hit those goals, I need to get my money working for me ASAP.

I didn't start to save a lot when I started making good money. Instead, I made a few conscious choices because principles are what matter. If you decide to eat out instead of making a sandwich at home, knowing your bank account balance is low, you won't be able to resist the urge to buy a new Audemars Piguet or Lamborghini when you have a lot in your account.

I'm not opposed to the nice things, and I will talk more about enjoying life because it is short; I'm just saying that early in your journey, it doesn't make sense. There will come a time when that Lamborghini makes you more money than it costs you— attracting sales reps, attracting clients, getting in the right room with others that can afford a Lambo, etc. One day, the payoff will be more than the payment. Stay patient, and don't force it. This is where I see so many people screw themselves over.

3. Savings Buckets

I want you to think of your savings account as a bucket. Each income stream you have is a hose that fills the bucket. Each liability, or expense, pokes a hole in your bucket. Some hoses and holes are bigger than others.

A house payment is likely a big hole in your bucket, but your primary income should be a big hose filling it back up. The goal is to have more going into the bucket than coming out of the holes.

Many people mess up once they get their bucket to a certain level and feel comfortable poking bigger holes in it because they have hoses filling it up. If they'd delay their gratification and the expenses that come with it for a couple of years, their bucket will overflow into another bucket, or they will be able to buy more hoses to fill their bucket more quickly.

That's a huge key to success: buy income.
Buy assets. Buy things that make you money.

Keep overflowing until you can't drain the bucket quickly enough because you have so many hoses filling it back up.

Especially if you're young.

Let's say you save up $100k—most younger salespeople would run out and buy a car. They would buy a house and increase their lifestyle to the point that $100k slowly becomes $90k saved up, then $50k. Then they would hover in that range.

And I get it; treat yourself. If you grew up poor and you've never seen that type of money, it's good to have nice stuff. But if you limit the nice stuff and continue to live below your means, that $100k invested could easily be worth way more in the future. If you spend it all immediately, you're doing yourself a huge disservice.

Once I started making money, I wanted a nice car and a nice watch—just those two things. But I told myself, *Zach, you can't get comfortable. Your goals are too big. You've got generational wealth to create, you have to make sure your family never worries about money again, and any money you spend now slows down your momentum.*

I realized it was easy to give in to the urges and cravings. It was hard keeping my lifestyle to a minimum, balancing treating myself a bit and enjoying life while saving and investing money until my passive income funds my lifestyle entirely.

That's the tipping point.

Most people make good money and think that means they can spend good money. I'd rather delay my gratification by saving and investing my money to change my family for generations.

> Every business needs customers and sales.
>
> Without those, you have a hobby, not a business.

This is what's necessary if you want to become financially free. And before you tell me wealth is luck or anything like that, here's a game plan for anybody: Let's say you make $50k a year, which almost anyone can do. Live below your means and use your spare time and money to learn a new skill that can produce more income. For me, this was sales, but it could be anything. You could sell someone else's nutritional products. You could flip tires and wheels. You could learn how to sell roofs in your free time. Find anything to put extra money into your pocket.

Once you learn the new skill, start a side hustle, focus, and make another $50k. Now you're at $100k—but don't see the additional $4k a month as "extra" money to spend. Instead, direct it into investments—maybe a rental house. Or get to a point with your side hustle where it can replace your main 9-5 gig you hate. Now, go all in on your side hustle and scale it to $100k since you have all your time directed toward it. That's the starting point; $100k is the minimum.

Keep living off a fraction of your income, increasing your income, and investing the extra money. If I were you, I'd buy real estate. My focus has shifted here after learning all the benefits and different ways to make money in real estate.

Real estate is the best investment you can make simply because of its many benefits.* I want to have a $25M real estate portfolio by the time I'm 30.

*This is not financial advice. Please do your due diligence and research.

If I own rentals, the tenants pay the mortgage down, which puts equity in my pocket. Also, houses appreciate and typically double in value roughly every ten years. I can do a cash-out refinance and pull the equity out tax-free while only putting 3.5-20% down while generating cash flow because rents increase consistently, and my mortgage is locked in at the same rate. Again, this is my opinion and is in no way meant to be taken as financial advice or fact.

That goal alone could take care of my family for generations to come. When you have big goals, delaying your gratification on the new Corvette or Rolex becomes easy even though you believe you deserve them.

Remember, I'm not saying I'll never get these things; I'm just saying I need to put my head down and delay it.

To be clear, I'm not against treating myself, nor do I cheap out on things I need. I understand the difference between being cheap and knowing the value of a dollar. I also understand that life is short. If you want something, treat yourself. I just find a compromise zone in treating myself to smaller gifts—and even then, I set a goal for myself to hit before buying it.

I mentioned Corvettes because I love them. If I didn't have huge goals and hadn't learned the value of a dollar from little Zach, I'd have a dark grey C7 Z06 parked outside my house right now—maybe even an all-black C8 with suicide doors.

But part of me is scared that once I own it, I won't be as happy or excited about it as I am thinking about the day I will finally get it—but that's another story.

Bottom line: I want this Corvette but don't want to drop $80k for it or pay $1600 a month. So what do I do?

And I want other things, too.

> Reverse-engineer your goals. Where do you want to be? How much money do you want to make? Learn the work it's going to take.

Stewman takes me to all his high-level masterminds, so I'm around some of the most successful entrepreneurs on the regular. At one of these events, I saw a few dudes wearing black Givenchy slides.

There we were, hanging out with dudes worth eight and nine figures, and they're wearing hoodies, joggers, and Givenchy slides.

I told y'all that I don't care about name brands too much, but these slides were TOUGH. Not to mention, these dudes got off on wearing a hoodie and joggers because they had nice slides and a nice watch. I loved the look and wanted a pair.

When I returned from California, I found some online and was just about to purchase them, but something about buying $300 shoes didn't sit right with me. It's just not who I am. So I told myself: *all right, Zach, you're good with your money, so let's treat yourself to these. But let's delay your gratification a couple of months and hit $800k in sales first. That way, this is a drop in the bucket.*

Two months passed, and I hit my goal and bought myself my reward. That was the carrot I set in front of myself.

It isn't worth it to me to purchase anything that I know decreases in value the minute I buy it. Instead, if I put that money into an investment, it will pay me for years, and eventually, the ROI will pay for what I want.

Do this, and you'll be amazed at how quickly you no longer desire the gift you wanted so badly.

Chapter 3

Money Makes Money

"And he shall be like a tree planted by the rivers of water, that bringeth forth his fruit in his season. His leaf also shall not wither; and whatsoever he doeth shall prosper."
–Psalm 1:3, KJV

The more money you put away, the more opportunities you will have to buy more hoses to fill your bucket more quickly.

I'm a huge advocate of multiple streams of income, passive and residual income, and ensuring your income is bulletproof—meaning your bills are covered every month.

As you grow your income, it's important to start thinking about the different types of investments out there. Real estate may be a great investment, but if I need to raise my income because I'm not at the level needed, that probably isn't the best initial investment.

Different investments are great for cash flow, building net worth, or both. Real estate could do both. But as I was coming up, I was focused on different types at different times.

> Stress relief – There's just something about knowing my bills are covered every single month. I think in a "this sale will pay for this" mindset. If I close a sale for $5000 per month and I know I get 10% of that every month, then I figure out what I can use that $500 to invest in or pay for something.

I'll give a glimpse into my investments, but understand that this is what I do; it is by no means financial advice.

At first, my focus was cash flow. I wanted to put $1 to work to bring me back $2. I created simple websites for local roofers, a tree service, and landscapers and made them show up first on Google. After they started bringing in leads, I'd rent the websites out to local businesses or build businesses around the website and arbitrage the leads.

> Make your bands with a main active income and invest your money into new income streams. Restaurants, rentals, businesses, etc.

The roofing leads went to my brother and his company. The tree service company became my own after I felt the tree guys I sent leads to did not appreciate them. I rented out the landscaping site.

These were great investments for me. Not only did I learn the game of digital marketing and building a business, but I also increased my cash flow. My whole time in college, I knew my bills were covered, even if I had to take a couple of months off from work to rush a fraternity. That's a significant milestone: having enough money from your investments to fund your life.

As I started working with Stewman and my income increased, I shifted my focus to investments. This is an important thing to note as well. So many people are against working for someone and want to own their stuff, but you can still have that entrepreneurial spirit to start side hustles and investments while using your main gig to pay your bills and set yourself up to build generational wealth.

At first, I would throw my money at anything with a good return: stocks, crypto, land investment deals, and bridge loans. It was all new to me, and seeing my money go out there and grow was cool. But then I saw this wasn't the best plan for me. I needed a better strategy than just throwing money out there and getting returns with various tax obligations at different times. I wanted a consistent investment that was the best for my goals, and at that point, my goal moved from cash flow to net worth.

You only need so much cash flow. Some of the most successful people I know who make millions of dollars only use about $40k per month, which is $480k per year—and that's on the high side—most spend more within the range of the $10k-20k mark.

I understand sales isn't for everyone, but if learning the skills to be successful in sales can make your life a lot easier. Sales is one of the few jobs with no income cap, doesn't require a college degree, and almost guarantees you'll always have food on your table. Of course, you can become wealthy working for someone else or in a salaried position. But consider putting in the time to develop the skills and don't let others tell you what your worth.

The name of the game is increasing your income to fuel your investments and supplement and eventually replace your full-time income.

Your goal is to become financially free.

It's not easy, but it is super simple. I'm going to break it down to be so simple that I know you will discount my opinion and think, *nah, that won't work for me.* It will. This is the way to not only make money but to become wealthy. To become financially free. To be the one person in your family who breaks generations of working for someone else doing things they don't want to do.

Step 1: Make money.

The best way to do this is to own a business or be self-employed and in sales. I highly recommend reading *The Greatest Salesman in the World,* which references the same opinion.

I fell in love with sales. Helping people and making a ton of money, who wouldn't love it? The KEY to sales is: simply to find a blue ocean and help people.

A blue ocean is a marketplace (the ocean) that doesn't yet have a lot of competition (sharks feeding in bloody water). That's what makes it blue.

> Don't focus on the payment. The payoff from being surrounded by the right people is much bigger.

But it should be called a green ocean because if you find a blue ocean and an irresistible offer that helps people where not too many people are fulfilling the need, you have the opportunity to make bank. I talk more about blue and red oceans in Chapter 6.

Remember, don't be average by not finishing the book.

Many people go into sales thinking all sales are the same, but they aren't. One hundred percent of the time, I'm buying the product or service that is best for me.

When it comes to insurance, other than price, there isn't much difference between salesman A and B. But if you are a broker and can guarantee the best policy and price for your customer, then you differentiate yourself from the other insurance salespeople who can only offer one policy.

So, Step 1 is to find a way to make money. I'd recommend sales, owning a business, or both, like me.

If you choose sales or business ownership, the next step is to find a blue ocean and an irresistible offer. Don't work on the side of a mountain and make it harder on yourself.

Find something you know makes sense once you get it in front of your ideal client. Apex is an irresistible offer to me. It's a coaching program and network that not only helps business owners and sales reps grow their business and sales, but it truly assists them in crushing every aspect of their lives. Apex is an absolute no-brainer when you consider its impact not only on me but on all our clients, which is why I sell millions of dollars of it every year.

Once I get in front of a sales rep wanting to close more deals, a business owner needing to work ON his business instead of IN his business, or an entrepreneur already doing seven, eight, or nine figures who wants to scale and hang around people doing things at a similar level, and tell them that Apex can help them do that while helping them make more money and surrounding themselves with a killer network to level up in every aspect of their life, it's an absolute no-brainer and an easy sale.

Another blue ocean I use to sell Apex is the tax services of one of my clients, Barbara.

Barbara saves entrepreneurs producing at very high-levels millions of dollars in taxes because she understands how the government wants to incentivize entrepreneurs to continue growing the economy.

I can sell clients our highest level of Apex by telling them that it may be possible to cover the annual Apex investment by connecting with Barbara to see how she can reduce their tax bills. THAT'S a blue ocean. Do you think Barbara struggles to sell her services to someone who made $10 million last year and is giving half of it to Uncle Sam after explaining that she can help them keep more? Of course not.

To recap, if you choose sales or entrepreneurship, your first step is finding an irresistible offer. If you choose to work for someone else, you should first ensure your salary is as high as possible and start looking for new ways to make money.

Step 2: Consistently earn a high income while keeping your lifestyle and expenses low.

Stack your bread.

The key to making money is surrounding yourself with the right people. If you're around people making $100k, you'll think that's the ceiling. But if your network earns millions, you'll believe $200-400k is just getting started.

When it comes to income, your first $100k is less powerful than your second because your first $100k has a lot of expenses tied to it: rent, food, and anything else you spend money on—all comes out of this $100k. So, it ends up being much less.

> Good is often the robber of great. $100k is good, but it won't get you too far ahead in life. You have to be willing to push past good, push past comfortable, to get to the disposable income, so you can start investing.

But that next $100k is profit because you don't have any expenses draining it. Besides Uncle Sam's cut, you are free to invest. So, that $100k is worth much more than $100k. If you invest it, it'll be $130k, but remember, you never stopped making money, so you still don't need it. Just live off the first $100k and use the additional money to start piecing together a financially free life that focuses on generational wealth. Once you start looking at it like that, you'll want another free $100k to invest.

Because I promise you $100k isn't the top. Too many people make that much per month or per day for you to think it's the best annual income you can have. That's why I'm such a huge advocate of learning a skillset: most jobs don't pay much more than $100k.

That's the power of starting early. I could put the first $1000 I made every month toward investing in myself and learning new skillsets while surrounding myself with better circles because I didn't have to worry about rent or food since I was 15 and still lived with my family.

I recently bought a house. My mortgage is $3100 per month, and I have three friends, each paying me $800 per month for a room. It's a good deal for them because it's $400 under market rent for a one bedroom in the area. They can save money while living with their best friends in an environment to grind and hustle. Together, they cover most of my mortgage, so I still live almost rent-free.

Sure I could live by myself—but it'd cost me a lot more money, and I'd much rather live with my buddies. It's a win-win.

One of the biggest keys to my success is being smart with my money and spending a lot less than I make. This is the easiest way to break you from the rat race and financial matrix.

Whether you make big money or little money, spend less than you make.

If you make little money, look for ways to cut back even more. If you make big money, don't buy that Lamborghini even though it'd be sick. Nobody expects a 22-year-old to have a Lamborghini. Why put your money toward that and drain your income when you could invest it today and buy the Lambo later *using the gains from your investment?*

Delay your gratification, and don't worry about what people think. Flex later, grind and invest now. Money and investing reward time. The biggest impact of compound interest (the interest you earn on interest) is time. Use it. Take advantage of getting a head start.

Case Study – $25 Million Real Estate Portfolio at 30

To achieve this goal, I need to buy two houses this year, three next year, five the following year, then eight every year until I'm 30. At an 8% appreciation rate and purchasing a new personal home with 5% down and investment homes with 20% down, I will need roughly $3.6 million invested over the next eight years to have a $25 million portfolio by the time I'm 30.

If I didn't buy another home after I turn 30, my portfolio would be $50 million when I'm 40 and $100 million when I'm 50, assuming an 8% appreciation rate.

If I continue to buy houses using cash flow and equity from appreciation on the original homes and continue making more money in my other businesses as they grow, which is inevitable, then I can fast forward my results even more through reinvestment and time of investment.

Column 1: Year

Column 2: Capital needed that year

Column 3: Down payment per house

Column 4: House price

Columns 5-14: Price of houses assuming 8% appreciation

1	2	3	4	5	6	7	8	9	10	11	12	13	14
Year	Capital needed this year	House Down Payment	House Value Initially	1	2	3	4	5	6	7	8	9	10
		20000	400000	432000	466560	503884.8	544195.584	587731.2307	634749.7292	685529.7075	740372.0841	799601.8508	863569.9989
1	80000	60000	300000	324000	349920	377913.6	408146.688	440798.423	476062.2969	514147.2806	555279.0631	599701.3881	647677.4992
		20000	400000		432000	466560	503884.8	544195.584	587731.2307	634749.7292	685529.7075	740372.0841	799601.8508
		60000	300000		324000	349920	377913.6	408146.688	440798.423	476062.2969	514147.2806	555279.0631	599701.3881
2	140000	60000	300000		324000	349920	377913.6	408146.688	440798.423	476062.2969	514147.2806	555279.0631	
		20000	400000			432000	466560	503884.8	544195.584	587731.2307	634749.7292	685529.7075	740372.0841
		60000	300000			324000	349920	377913.6	408146.688	440798.423	476062.2969	514147.2806	555279.0631
		60000	300000			324000	349920	377913.6	408146.688	440798.423	476062.2969	514147.2806	555279.0631
3	260000	60000	300000			324000	349920	377913.6	408146.688	440798.423	476062.2969	514147.2806	555279.0631
		25000	500000				540000	583200	629856	680244.48	734664.0384	793437.1615	856912.1344
		60000	300000				324000	349920	377913.6	408146.688	440798.423	476062.2969	514147.2806
		60000	300000				324000	349920	377913.6	408146.688	440798.423	476062.2969	514147.2806
		60000	300000				324000	349920	377913.6	408146.688	440798.423	476062.2969	514147.2806
		60000	300000				324000	349920	377913.6	408146.688	440798.423	476062.2969	514147.2806
		60000	300000				324000	349920	377913.6	408146.688	440798.423	476062.2969	514147.2806
4	445000	60000	300000				324000	349920	377913.6	408146.688	440798.423	476062.2969	514147.2806
		25000	500000					540000	583200	629856	680244.48	734664.0384	793437.1615
		60000	300000					324000	349920	377913.6	408146.688	440798.423	476062.2969
		60000	300000					324000	349920	377913.6	408146.688	440798.423	476062.2969
		60000	300000					324000	349920	377913.6	408146.688	440798.423	476062.2969
		60000	300000					324000	349920	377913.6	408146.688	440798.423	476062.2969
		60000	300000					324000	349920	377913.6	408146.688	440798.423	476062.2969
5	445000	60000	300000					324000	349920	377913.6	408146.688	440798.423	476062.2969
		25000	500000						540000	583200	629856	680244.48	734664.0384
		60000	300000						324000	349920	377913.6	408146.688	440798.423
		60000	300000						324000	349920	377913.6	408146.688	440798.423
		60000	300000						324000	349920	377913.6	408146.688	440798.423
		60000	300000						324000	349920	377913.6	408146.688	440798.423
		60000	300000						324000	349920	377913.6	408146.688	440798.423
6	445000	60000	300000						324000	349920	377913.6	408146.688	440798.423
		25000	500000							540000	583200	629856	680244.48
		60000	300000							324000	349920	377913.6	408146.688
		60000	300000							324000	349920	377913.6	408146.688
		60000	300000							324000	349920	377913.6	408146.688
		60000	300000							324000	349920	377913.6	408146.688
		60000	300000							324000	349920	377913.6	408146.688

1	2	3	4	5	6	7	8	9	10	11	12	13	14
Year	Capital needed this year	House Down Payment	House Value Initially	1	2	3	4	5	6	7	8	9	10
		60000	300000							324000	349920	377913.6	408146.688
7	445003	60000	300000							324000	349920	377913.6	408146.688
		25000	500000								540000	583200	629856
		60000	300000								324000	349920	377913.6
		60000	300000								324000	349920	377913.6
		60000	300000								324000	349920	377913.6
		60000	300000								324000	349920	377913.6
		60000	300000								324000	349920	377913.6
8	445000	60000	300000								324000	349920	377913.6
		25000	500000									540000	583200
		60000	300000									324000	349920
		60000	300000									324000	349920
		60000	300000									324000	349920
		60000	300000									324000	349920
		60000	300000									324000	349920
		60000	300000									324000	349920
9	445000	60000	300000									324000	349920
		25000	500000										540000
		60000	300000										324000
		60000	300000										324000
		60000	300000										324000
		60000	300000										324000
		60000	300000										324000
		60000	300000										540000
10	445000	60000	300000										324000
		60000	300000										
		60000	300000										
		60000	300000										
		60000	300000										
		60000	300000										
		60000	300000										
		60000	300000										
		60000	300000										
		60000	300000										
		60000	300000										
		60000	300000										
		60000	300000										
		60000	300000										
		60000	300000										
		60000	300000										
		60000	300000										
		60000	300000										

Total Capital needed in order to grow a total portfolio of $31.7M by the time I'm 30.

Total Capital Needed	Portfolio Size
3,595,000	$ 31,742,972

Chapter 4

Lesson from My Dad: Hard Work is Key

*"When you do more than you're paid for,
eventually, you'll be paid for more than you do."*
–Zig Ziglar

This is the lesson I am most grateful to have learned.

Learning how money works will allow me to make a lot, invest a lot, donate a lot, and change my family's life for generations. But imagine the families I'll be able to change by providing jobs and donating money to charities.

Imagine the people reading this book who weren't able to be in the rooms I've been in who learned something new about the way money works. Imagine the amount of money they'll make, invest, and donate. That's the power of money.

Money allows you to be free and help others, and I am forever grateful I learned how it works. But again, that's not the lesson I'm most grateful to have learned.

Two horses were carrying two loads. The front horse carried well, but the rear horse was lazy. The men began to pile the rear horse's load on the front horse. When they had transferred it all, the rear horse found it easy-going, and he said to the front horse, "Toil and sweat! The more you try, the more you have to suffer."
When they reached the tavern, the owner said, "Why should I fodder two horses when I can carry all on one? I had better give the one all the food it wants, and cut the throat of the other. At least I shall have the hide." And so he did.
FABLES, LEO TOLSTOY, 1828-1910
(As quoted in 'The 48 Laws of Power' by Robert Greene)
https://simerjeet.wordpress.com/2013/11/19/the-fable-of-the-two-horses/

I'm most grateful to have learned that *being the hardest worker in the room will always get you what you want in life.*

The struggle is what rewards us.

No matter what I do in my life, I always strive to be the hardest worker. I take pride in outworking everyone around me. It's easy for someone to say, "Oh, he got lucky." What's hard is doing the work required to reach a level of success where people feel they need to tear you down by making it seem like your hard work was luck.

Every overnight success takes years.
People always forget the late nights and early mornings,
so they call you an overnight success.

Hard work.

It all started in my childhood. I would see my dad working his tail end off. He was always the hardest worker at work, at home, and everywhere else. I wanted to be just like him and always looked for his recognition. I'd see him mowing the lawn and go out there to help, even when I wasn't old enough. I'd still get him water and hang out in the 100-degree Texas heat. I enjoyed doing the hard stuff.

Chores? Help the most at home and make your parents happy. That work ethic will impact every aspect of your life.

School group project? Be the person that contributes the most to the project. Carry the weight.

Sports? Be the most knowledgeable and hardest worker on the field. Make sure your teammates know they can rely on you.

The biggest opportunity I've had? An internship with Ryan Stewman. Come in as an intern and be the hardest worker. Show them you can provide more value than a $15/hr. internship. Show them you're different and want to move up, unlike the average 19-year-old.

It all comes down to being willing to work harder than everyone else and truly taking pride in it.

I'm not sure if I'm different from most people in that hard work comes naturally to me. I love working hard. I cannot sit around and do nothing. I can't be average; I hate everything about average. I always have to go above and beyond and work as hard as possible—and I owe that personality trait to my dad.

It's so easy to discredit someone's success by saying they are lucky, but the truth is that it's hard not to be successful when you are consistently working harder than others and consistently taking pride in doing the work, when you are consistently operating at a higher level.

> Be more invested into your people's dreams. They don't care about the paycheck. They care about what the paycheck buys them: a new house, a new car, an investment, etc.

If I had to give credit for all my success up to this point and identify one attribute, it would 100% be my work ethic.

My dad got me the opportunity to be in the room with Stewman as an intern since he'd been a client for years, but it was on me to take it from there. Did I want to stay making $15 per hour and grabbing lunch for everyone in the office, or did I want to become a top sales producer, so I could do what I wanted?

I had to outwork everyone in the office to earn respect and catch up to other sales reps who had been there longer than me; they had renewals coming in and were already the "go-to." I had to work overtime. But people don't want to talk about that—they'd rather call me lucky.

I had to work weekends training our roofing sales reps when I was dead tired after working 80-hour weeks with Stewman. But people don't want to talk about that—they'd rather call me lucky.

> Your job as a leader is to get more out of your people than they can get out of themselves. If you can create leaders, you can impact ten times as many people.

I spent hours learning about SEO and building websites to create my tree service business while generating leads for our roofing company. I missed out on a ton of high school memories, and people made fun of me for going all-in on digital marketing, but they don't want to talk about that—they'd rather call me lucky.

I'm investing hundreds of thousands of dollars into real estate that will make me more money in appreciation than the average household makes per year in America. But the only way I got that money was from grinding to learn sales, becoming the best at it, starting companies, scaling companies, working when I'm tired, and working harder than everyone else.

The point I'm trying to make is: if you are seriously willing to work harder than everyone else, there is absolutely no way you won't be successful. Yes, you'll have to think smarter too, but hard work is necessary. "Work smarter, not harder" has become a popular phrase, but while those people sit back and slack as they "work smarter," I'm doing both and running circles around them.

Hard work truly is the greatest equalizer.

Do more work than every other person out there. When your competition rests, you work more. When they work hard, you work harder. The key is working harder than everyone else.

I believe that if you are truly willing to do the work, nothing is stopping you from being successful. I've seen too many entrepreneurs, athletes, and others come from absolutely nothing, realize they want to be worth something, and work as hard as possible to get there.

> There are levels to this game. Once you think you've 'made' it is when you'll tap out and stop growing. What got you to one level won't get you to the next room. The goal is to outgrow the room, then find a bigger room.

Growing up without money is just as advantageous as growing up with it. Some may even argue that growing up without money is better. Sure, you might not go to college, but you get four years to learn real-world experience. Maybe you won't get the connections at the country club, but you can see what the bottom looks like and decide whether you want to stay there. That decision can be enough to turn you into a dog and make you become the hardest worker in the room.

I see more first-generation successful people than multi-generational. Maybe I'm just in different rooms, or perhaps it's just my Reticular Activating System showing me what I focus on. But I see more people willing to work hard who come from the bottom and change their generational lineage simply from having that drive and work ethic. You can see it in athletes, rappers, and blue-collar millionaires. If you come from nothing, you have a huge advantage. You just have to realize it. Once you do, **your work ethic will be the ultimate equalizer, and you'll quickly catch up to those who grew up with millions.**

I'm writing this book seven years into doing the work. That's seven years of focusing on being the hardest worker in the room. I can only imagine where 20 years of consistent work will get me.

I won't drag this chapter out longer than it needs to be. It's my #1 secret to my success, but it's also the simplest, so I knew it belonged in this book:

Do the work.

Do the work despite the excuses.

Despite the feelings.

Whether you feel like it or not.

Do the work and have that discipline, and you will be grateful that you did.

Chapter 5

Ryan Stewman:
Winning in Every Aspect of Your Life

"Some people are so poor all they have is money."
–Bob Marley

I read *GCode: How to Stay Super Focused in a World Full of Distractions* by my mentor Ryan Stewman. In Chapter 3, Ryan walks you through the most powerful exercise I've ever done. (You can find that exercise at ZachSasser1.PhoneSites.com.) That one chapter has been responsible for thousands of happy days when I used just to let days pass me by, hundreds of thousands of dollars in sales when I used to just go through the motions to make sales, tons of my most powerful relationships by being intentional with them, and a body that I look at in the mirror every day proud that I put the work in to achieve it.

Ryan has been one of the most instrumental humans in my life. He has extracted more greatness out of me than I knew possible. That is what a true leader does: holds you to your potential more than you can yourself. This dude has done more to change my life and show me what's possible than anybody else.

He's taught me the world of business, sure. But more importantly, he's taught me what it truly looks like to win in life, not only in finances. If we're being honest, money isn't hard to make. Once you start researching and educating yourself, acquire the skills needed, and under-

> A closer is somebody who asks powerful questions that challenge the traditional paradigm of thinking.

stand how capitalism and society work, it's pretty simple. What's hard is winning in every aspect of your life. Winning doesn't mean being in the office 12 hours a day, having no genuine relationships, being overweight, and wanting to kill yourself.

The GCode program, as covered in the book, is a way of structuring and being very intentional with how you live your life. It's about being great in the four areas of your life that matter most:

1. Gratitude (mindset)

2. Genetics (health)

3. Grind (work, finances)

4. Group (the people you surround yourself with).

So many people let time pass them by without making any progress toward their goals. Sometimes they don't even know what their goals are. They just passively play at life.

Forget that.

I've got one shot at living the best life I possibly can. One body to mold into the greatest possible version of myself that it can be. You're crazy if you think I'm not going to make sure I live the life I want, that I won't give myself the mindset I want, the body and health I want, the career and money I want, and the people I want in my life.

Call me selfish, but I want to make sure this one shot I have in life is the best one I can possibly make. I want to become the person God put me on this planet to become. I want to impact as many people as possible and not be restrained from doing what I want when I want because of a lack of financial or time freedom.

I hope people look at me and say, "I want his mindset and outlook on life. I want my body to look like his and to be as healthy as him. I want his financial status and to be able to do what I want with my time like he does. I want his relationships and to care about people and have people care about me as much as they care about him."

My #1 mission in life is to become the most elite version of myself and to help as many people as possible become the greatest versions of themselves.

> If you're not where you want to be, it's because you're not who you need to be right now.

Right now, I believe the best way for me to do that is to inspire and show people what's possible. Eventually, I'm sure it will include teaching people what I learned to become successful. There is so much knowledge and wisdom available on everything you want to accomplish. Unfortunately, most people are unaware, so they're stuck in mediocrity and stay average.

I hate average.

I don't want anything to do with average.

I want to help people break from being average and become the most elite version of themselves.

The best way I know how to do that is through the Greatness Code that my biggest mentor, Ryan Stewman, instilled in me.

4 G's. Ryan taught me that if you focus on these four areas of your life every day, you will become the greatest version of yourself.

G1: Gratitude

This is your mindset. Everything in life starts with gratitude. Since I have started intentionally telling myself that I am grateful for everything in my life, everything has changed.

That sounds like a tall order, but I believe there is a reason Ryan put this as the very first G of the G-Code.

Think about the power you hold, knowing that nobody can break your spirit because you're grateful no matter what they do to you. If I'm driving down the highway and someone cuts me off, the old me would've yelled at them, probably gotten into the next lane over, and sped in front of them just to show them nobody gets one over on me—as if it gave me some sort of power. But ever since gratitude has become a focus, I keep driving and don't let it influence my life.

I'm grateful even to have a car when so many people don't. I'm grateful to have a destination worth going to, whether it be seeing my family or driving to sign a deal. I'm grateful that the driver didn't cause us to get into a wreck. But even if they did, I'd be grateful that I didn't die and that I have insurance to cover the damages and the skills to make more money to buy an even better truck.

Do you see how powerful this is yet?

Another scenario. Someone has been stealing money from you for years. Your first instinct is to be mad, to want to fight them, and get your money back. And sure, get your money back if possible. But don't get too wound up and allow it to throw you off your game. Be grateful you found out before they stole more. Be grateful you were making enough money for it not to be a big deal that they were stealing from you all those years. Be grateful you found out now instead of after another ten years.

I'm not saying that you should be oblivious to bad things happening to you. I'm just saying that bad things are going to happen, and a lot of the time, you can't control when they do. So why spend that time stressing, being mad, and letting that person or situation control you? Focus on what you can control and be grateful for everything in life.

The best way to do that is to go to GCode.PhoneSites.com and take the zero to 100 challenge. It's free (even though Ryan should charge for it because people take things more seriously when they pay for them). Give it 30 days and see if you notice a difference. I guarantee you will; it's made all the difference for me.

G2: Genetics

This is your fitness and diet. Do you work out and stick to a diet?

It doesn't have to be two-a-day workouts, and it doesn't have to be chicken, rice, and broccoli. But it does have to complement your fitness goals. You can have all the money in the world, but if you are unhealthy or out of shape and stuck in a hospital bed at 60, you aren't living your best life.

Growing up, I played sports. Every once in a while, I'd roll my ankle while playing, and it wasn't until then that I realized how much I take for granted a healthy ankle. The same goes for my health. Every time I get sick, I realize how much I take for granted being healthy. I know it's going to be the same when I'm old and my body can't heal itself as well. So why not get ahead of that by practicing health and fitness now?

I've always been a huge advocate for working out. It's been a stress release and therapy for me, so lifting weights has never been a chore. I've struggled with the diet portion, and the GCode helps me stick to a diet to reach my fitness and body goals. Working out is great, but if you're naturally skinny like me, you know how hard it is to put on mass. Overweight people are probably saying the grass is always greener, but the truth is both are hard. Your diet is responsible for your gains way more than the work you do in the gym.

I'm not here to tell you to get in shape, even though I think it's crucial to live your best life. I want to convey that a daily focus on health and diet has significantly helped me become the greatest version of myself, and I know it can do the same for you.

G3: Grind

Money isn't everything, but it's pretty important. You can't even buy the water you need to live without money. "Grind" is about more than just making money; it's about doing something you genuinely love and are passionate about.

I have a few different roles right now. My primary role is sales for Ryan and our Apex program. I'm not in a cubicle calling people who don't want to hear from me all day. I'm creating content and helping people win so much in their businesses and life that they go out and tell their friends, and I sign them up as well.

If you were to tell me that I'd get paid hundreds of thousands of dollars to sell a life-changing product, be surrounded by hundreds of millionaires who will pour into me, and make sure I reach those numbers much faster than they did—while working on improving in every aspect of my life and running side businesses, investing my money, and setting my hours—I wouldn't have believed you. But I found a way to make a living while enjoying what I do every single day. And that's what it's all about.

> Don't only focus on making money; learn the tax code to keep your money.

But don't stop there. As we learned in Chapter 2, you want more than one income. Start a side hustle. Vertically integrate your companies. Keep growing your income and businesses.

That's what G3 is about: never having to stress about your finances.

G4: Group

This represents the people you surround yourself with. Ryan says, "Your alignment takes precedent over your assignment," meaning who you are with is more important than what you do in life.

> Energy is contagious. You will become who you surround yourself with.

Once you surround yourself with the right people, you start learning the right things. You start meeting the right people. You start getting the right opportunities.

But the opposite is true, too. Our mamas always told us, "Don't hang out with those kids; they're trouble." As much as we hate to admit it, mama is always right. Every time you started hanging around the wrong people, you got into trouble.

The saying that you are who you hang out with could not be any closer to the truth. More than anything else, this is what has changed my life the most since working with Ryan.

I started working under Ryan as an Intrapreneur at 19. If you don't know him, he runs one of the largest, most powerful business networks. I'm talking about people who make hundreds of millions; there are even a couple of billionaires. You'll find people winning not just in business and finances—they are truly winning in every aspect of their lives:

People with happy families and a date night every week.

People in shape, in the gym 4-5 times a week.

Fathers leading their families.

Mothers leading their families.

Winning in every aspect of their life.

When I was surrounded by this network at 19, I literally had no choice but to be successful.

When you're having conversations with people like Brandon Brittingham and Keith Pike, learning how they're the top real estate brokers and team leads in the country, when you're talking with people who own multiple businesses, who are vertically integrating, quadrupling commissions, and owning hundreds of rental properties, you start to truly see what's possible.

You learn how wealth works.

You learn how to win in every aspect of your life.

You learn how to kill it in sales, level up as a business owner, invest your money, and save on taxes by setting up an LLC and then electing to be taxed as an S-Corp (this is not financial advice; please act as if everything I say is fictional).

You learn everything you need to know.

You have a support system.

You are surrounded by people who understand, motivate, and push you.

You become who you surround yourself with, and being surrounded by Ryan's Apex network has completely changed who I was and what I could accomplish.

If you are interested in growing into the greatest version of yourself, killing it in sales, working on your business instead of in your business to scale—or you already run an 8-, 9-, or even 10-figure business—I highly recommend you join Apex. I've been a part of tons of masterminds or coaching programs that promise the world, but Apex is the only one I've seen consistently help their clients grow into the greatest versions of themselves time and time again. That's the only reason I rock with them so hard.

I got my nickname "Young Closer" by being the top producer for Apex at only 21 years old. I have other companies that I run, but selling Apex is my main focus. But the cool thing about it is that I'm not the only success story in Apex. I'm the poster child, but all our clients are winning. Our clients win so big in Apex that they don't ever leave us.

We have clients who have been around for years, renewing year after year because we help them win in every aspect of their lives and make way more money than they pay us, so it makes no sense for them to leave us.

If you would like to learn more about Apex, visit: ZachSasser1.PhoneSites.com.

It's an understatement to say that this program has changed my life.

Being surrounded by the right people is important to your success; that's another understatement. The goal is to be the smallest fish in the pond. Get in a room where people are so successful that you feel uncomfortable.

Imagine being 19, still in college, not having $10k to your name, and being surrounded by bosses. Actual bosses. Not the ones who fake it on Instagram. I'm talking about people who are writing for Forbes, listed as the #1 RE/MAX broker, and accredited investors making stupid money. They aren't only rich; they're wealthy.

Being surrounded by this many high producers made me uncomfortable. If you want to talk about impostor syndrome, imagine how I felt. I knew I'd be on their level one day, but I was still just starting. But instead of

> You will have to become a new version of yourself to reach the next level. What got you here won't get you there. It all falls on you. Everything rises and falls on leadership.

staying scared, I chose to use that fear and discomfort to level up. I used the knowledge I learned when LISTENING to their conversations and actually implemented it in my own businesses to build 7-, soon to be 8-figure businesses.

Chapter 6

Dan Klein: Scaling

"Leverage is the reason some people become
rich and others do not become rich."
–Robert Kiyosaki

Dan Klein taught me one of the foundational pieces of my career and entrepreneurial journey. When you first get exposed to the entrepreneurial path, it seems like an endless rabbit hole, and it's honestly terrifying. You have no skills and no idea what to even focus on.

You're learning all these weird new buzzwords and what they mean: personal development, e-com, social media marketing, email lists, drop shipping, sub-to, wholesaling, etc. You have no idea about sales, marketing, taxes, legal, or anything else. You see all the possibilities but don't really know where to start.

Focus is a superpower.
—Ryan Stewman

Until you know which direction you want to go and can focus on it—truly focus on becoming an expert, truly focus on what's needed to become successful—you're going to spin your wheels. This is when I say, "Doing anything is better than doing nothing," If you don't start doing, you won't know what you like or don't like, and you won't acquire any skills.

I truly believe God will tell you everything you're supposed to do, but he won't do it for you. He won't make you brave; He'll give you an opportunity to be brave. He won't make you fearless; He'll give you an opportunity to become fearless. He won't make you a leader; He'll give you an opportunity to be a leader. And He won't make you successful; He'll give you an opportunity to be successful.

Go mess up. Start something, mess it up, keep going, figure out what you like and don't like. It's all healthy, and it's all necessary for success.

The world is huge. Especially if you're a young entrepreneur like me, who is learning not only about the entrepreneur world but also about how the world works in general. The best thing you can do is keep trying things and then find something to focus on.

Dan Klein provided me with the focus to get started. Not only did Dan give me a clear place to start, but he also gave me the skill set to start crushing it. I'll dive into how this happened in a second, and I'll tell you how, without the skills I learned from Dan, I would never have taken off with Stewman the way I did. But the biggest lessons Dan taught me were the power of inbound marketing and the power of being able to scale.

Storytime!

I told y'all in the opening chapter that I was exposed to marketing and building a company at a young age. There was so much to learn in the beginning that it took a lot of time to start making headway within my company, but what really set it off was learning what Dan teaches.

Dan teaches how to create super simple websites online with generic titles, such as "Tree Service in Dallas TX," then make those websites show up first on Google when someone searches for a tree service company in Dallas.

Next, there are multiple ways to monetize the leads. The most common is to rent that website out to an actual tree service company in the area since you don't want to have to cut the trees. I tried that, but I realized there were greater margins if I used the leads myself. So, I started a tree service company; I created roofing sites for my family roofing company, and had sites for other companies around us.

The sites were awesome, and I still have them up today, bringing in money every month. The tree service company does six figures on autopilot, as I hired my mom to coordinate, and she crushes it. The roofing sites bring in 5-figure deals regularly. But the biggest thing these sites taught me was the power of scale.

You can only do so much yourself.

If you work for a wage, you have to actually work for an hour to get paid for that hour. There is no scale in that arrangement because if you don't show up to work, you don't get paid. You have to find a way to get paid without the amount you're paid being tied to an hourly wage. People always look for "high-paying jobs" when they should look for high-paying skills. Once you learn a high-paying skill, you can turn it into a high-paying job. But looking for a high-paying salary job is an uphill battle. Even if you find one, you may find out you don't want it.

But imagine if you could get paid whether you showed up for an hour or not. Imagine if you detached getting paid from the time you spent working.

I made those sites years ago, and they still bring in money for me. They're such simple sites—they might've taken me 20 hours to make when I was still learning the process, but once I made one, I could duplicate the site, change the words, and have another site within hours. If I were to add up all the income those sites have brought in over the past years, those hours would be worth thousands of dollars. Forget a $15 per hour job; I'd rather spend an hour of my time building something that will pay me over and over and over again.

**No truly wealthy person got that way by having someone else
tell them what their time was worth. They found a way to scale.**

You absolutely have to find a way to scale.

> Think long-
> term. You
> want your job
> to get easier.

Whether it be by getting good at a craft (like sales), helping others succeed in return for an override off them, automating a process such as lead generation like my websites, or doing something else entirely, the point is you have to find a way to detach your income from the amount of time or hours you put in.

MLMs do this. Automations do this. You can do this with any business where you hire people under you.

My brother's roofing company does this. At the time of the writing of this chapter, we have ten sales reps on our team. By teaching these sales reps how to make hundreds of thousands of dollars by selling a roof, not only do I help them make more money than they've ever made and learn a skill that they didn't have or weren't as good at, but their work allows us to scale, too.

**It's a win-win, and win-wins are what
make the business world go around.**

We even allow our sales reps to turn into team leads so they can eventually make a couple hundred thousand dollars by themselves. But they can also make a couple hundred thousand by training and being responsible for their team's production. It's like creating businesses inside of a business.

You have to do it first, so you're an expert. Then you have to teach others how to do it and get them to a point where they can hire and train others and build people under them.

That's the best way. Learn it, do it, teach it.

Dan also taught me about blue oceans. As I mentioned, blue oceans are what so many people miss in marketing. This causes a ton of frustration and forces people to battle uphill. A blue ocean is an area of the market you can dominate. Here, you have a unique advantage or something that sets you apart from everyone else in that industry or market.

This phrase comes from a book titled *Blue Ocean Strategy* by Renée Mauborgne and W. Chan Kim. I first learned about it in another book, *Expert Secrets* by Russell Brunson, when the authors compared the marketplace to an ocean.

The authors were saying that there are a bunch of sharks trying to find food in the ocean. Whenever a lot of sharks are feeding off the same fish, the water gets bloodied and turns red. Your goal should be to find or create an ocean where nobody is competing, meaning there is no blood in the water because all the fish are not being eaten.

The blue ocean we searched for was dominating Google search rankings by looking for the low-hanging fruit. It isn't the lazy way; it's the smart way. The SEO process takes time and can be harder in some markets than others. Why spend six years trying to rank in one market when you can spend six months and rank in another?

This applies to many areas. I see people hop into different sales industries and fight so hard. But if they only took inventory of where they were and what blue markets existed, they could fast-forward their results.

Creating a Blue Ocean from a Bloody Ocean

I don't want to talk bad about any industry because I know people who are successful in all of them, especially insurance—but if I were to sell insurance, here's how I'd do it:

Everyone needs insurance, but nobody really wants it. It's a boring and long process to get it, so once you do, you usually stay with the same company for years. If I wanted to dominate the insurance process, I would look at what my customer wants: the best policy possible to cover their needs at the lowest price. But they don't want a complicated and lengthy process to switch companies.

Also, I'd work for a brokerage rather than a typical insurance company that offers only its own policies. This way, I could shop around for the best policy and price to meet each client's unique needs. I could guarantee that I would save them money and increase their coverage. *Why would you not do it?*

One objection would be not wanting to deal with the long, stressful process of switching. They'd have to call their current company, cancel their policy, and get set up with the new one. Nobody has time for that.

Problems are what make us problem-solvers money.

I'd streamline this process to make it as simple as I could. *How can I cancel their existing policy and get them on the new one as easily as possible?* If I could save them thousands every year, or even hundreds, while getting them a better policy, all within an hour, who would say no to that?

If you know how to craft an irresistible offer in a blue ocean market, you will dominate it in sales and business. This is where I see so many people struggle. Don't make your sale hard; make it easy.

Here's how I crush it in life and business by creating irresistible offers:

Apex: As a reminder, Apex is a coaching and business networking program that helps salespeople and business owners level up not only financially but in every aspect of their lives. We give you the training to increase your sales, start working *on* your business instead of *in* your business, or scale your business even more while surrounding you with hundreds of millionaires —people who are winning in life and are willing to pour into you to help you fast-forward your success, just like they have for me.

That's an irresistible offer and a blue ocean in an industry where if people thought like marketers rather than salespeople, they'd make a killing.
I know multiple people in our Apex Executives program who do exactly that, and they crush it.

If you are a salesperson or business owner who wants to grow, and I tell you we can help you do exactly that in every aspect of your life while making more money than the program costs, could you say no to that?

It definitely makes it tough. I'm not saying I don't get no's. Not everybody is my ideal client, and that is perfectly fine with me. It's my job to get that offer in front of the right people.

The cool part here is that doctors hang out with doctors, football players hang out with football players, and my ideal client hangs around even more of my ideal clients.

Example

Lonestar Exterior: I've got two irresistible offers on this one—one for recruiting sales reps to our company and one for our customers.

> Recruiting: Lonestar Exterior is a roofing company, but more than that, it is an opportunity to surround yourself with a culture of young hustlers making a lot of money while learning how to crush it in business and life. Not only will we give you the skillset of sales (once you have it, you will never have to worry about having a job again), but we will help you make a lot of money, save on taxes, and invest your money—all while being surrounded by a culture of growth and personal development.

> If you want to make more money, look forward to going to work, and do what not many others out there are, we'd love to see if you'd fit in with our culture and core values.

> Homeowners: Nobody wants to deal with replacing their roof. It can be a complicated and expensive process, especially in Texas, because we often get hit with hail. There are so many bad roofing companies out there that it isn't hard to stand out when you're one of the good ones. We will help make this process as easy and painless as possible while ensuring your most precious asset is protected and taken care of as if it were our own. We treat you like family. We walk you through and will handle every step of the process to make sure nothing gets skipped or left out, all at an unbeatable price. That's just good business right there.

Once I truly learned the power of simply understanding what your ideal client wants and needs in your product and targeting that by forming irresistible offers, life became easier.

This applies to more than just business. What does the girl or guy of your dreams want?

Write down who your ideal spouse is. What do they like? What time do they get up? What do they do during the day? Who do they hang out with? What type of music do y'all listen to together? Everything. Write it all down.

Now, write down who your ideal spouse is attracted to **and become that person**.

If your ideal spouse is a smokeshow, she's not going to want a guy who's overweight—so you better make sure you're in shape. If she's going to be a great mom, she's not going to want to be with a man who comes home from work angry or too tired to contribute.

The power move is to become what they want, making it way easier to close them. This works whether they are a client, employee, or even girlfriend or boyfriend.

If you know how to market yourself and get in front of the right people, and know how to sell yourself and your product, you will never go hungry. There will always be money coming. There will always be food on your table, and you will never have to worry about having a job again.

You will be the most powerful person in the marketplace. Take the time to learn and master those skills.

Chapter 7

Jose: You Need an Enemy

"Without a worthy opponent,
a man or group cannot grow stronger."
–Robert Greene

Setting goals and having enemies are crucial to hitting the next level.

In life, it's easy to get complacent, especially when you're winning. But to break free from where you are currently, you must put your back against the wall.

One of the biggest cheat codes I use to reach the next level of success is to set huge goals and picture an enemy.

I talked about my most recent internship with Ryan Stewman turning into me becoming his top producer. It took about six months for me to go from intern to sales, then another six months to really start putting up numbers. I was a year into it when I started getting attention. That was when one of the smartest dudes I've ever met—Jose—called me on my stuff.

"You're too complacent," he told me. "You're 21, making more money than any of the people you're around, and you're happy there. That's the reason you haven't become the top producer, and why you're holding yourself back from your true potential."

That was all I needed to hear.

Over years of being around MFs way smarter than me, I have learned how to ask the right questions. Asking the right questions is an underrated skill and correlates directly to closing more sales. "All right, how do I reach that next level?" I asked him.

"You need an enemy. You need someone that has doubted you. Someone that hates you or acts like they want you to win, but you know it's a façade. If you don't have an enemy right now, create one. Enemies keep you sharp. Enemies make you focus. They fuel you, and that's exactly what you need to hit the next level."

Done.

One of the hardest lessons I've learned along this journey is that people don't want you to win. As much as you'd think your friends and family would want you to succeed, things get a little weird once you start winning. As soon as you step out of the status quo and truly create something for yourself and do something different to get a different result, many of your supporters become haters.

And there are levels to this.

The first group of people hate from the beginning and lets you know they don't like you doing great things. The second group switches up midjourney. Although they are supportive at first, they don't want you to win more than them.

Group one has a "crabs in a bucket" mentality. I saw this as I started posting more content and became a creator instead of a consumer. It was as clear as day who supported me and who made fun of me.

I don't believe they do this because they don't want you to be successful. You are in the same position as them, so if you break free, change your habits, and become successful, and they don't, they have to face the fact that maybe they are leaving a lot of their potential on the table. They hate you for showing them they have no excuse not to be successful.

Keep in mind that I was in college when I started posting content. So, while I was rushing a fraternity and had all these new people figuring out who I was—most of them worrying about partying and doing typical college things—I was busy messing up and posting terrible content because you're never good when you first start. I had many haters.

This was easy to get past when I looked at the lives of those haters right off the bat and realized there was a reason they hated me. They weren't happy with their lives, and I wouldn't be happy if I had their lives either. That kind of hater shook me for a minute, but I got over it quickly.

The second group of haters shook me for a bit longer.

These people support you for a while; then, they become haters. They cheer you on until you start winning more than them, and they see you as a threat. I got past the lame kids hating on my content and moved into this second set of people who I made my enemies. I had two specifically.

The first was an enemy I'd created about six months earlier when I planned to take a mentor in my life out for a nice steak dinner to show my appreciation for pouring so much knowledge into me and helping me get started. Another dude invited himself, which was fine because I looked up to him a ton, too. I thought he was cool, so I said yes, but once we got there, he started fueling me by turning himself into my enemy.

He said things like, "You haven't done anything," and "You shouldn't be happy with where you are at. You haven't done anything notable."

I know that he might have meant what he said in a motivational or supportive way, but it didn't sound like it—and it's not how a 21-year-old would have taken "You haven't done anything, kid."

I got defensive. "What do you think I'm trying to do, dude? I know you're 40 and been in the game longer than me, but you started somewhere."

Regardless of how he meant it, I'm grateful he said it because it fueled me, especially as I started to match his biggest life achievements as a 22-year-old top producer and 7-figure business owner when it took him 40 years to do the same. We ain't the same, bro.

All men are created equal.
Some just work harder in preseason.
–Unknown

Creating an Enemy

The next job was to create another enemy.

Simple—the dude in front of me in sales. I didn't hate him; I actually liked him even when he was my enemy. I just needed to fuel that healthy competition by viewing him as an enemy. It kept me sharp and gave me a number to hit every month.

Jose and I had been going through some stuff in our personal lives for a few months, which helped grow our bond. Having someone experience some deep stuff with you at the same time builds a powerful connection.

We met up every morning to hit the gym and had lunch together every day. That was my dude and still is.

It took a month between the moment Jose told me to find an enemy and when Ryan congratulated me on being the top producer for Apex. That's when I realized the power of having an enemy.

During that time, I was more focused than ever on hitting a goal. I learned how to channel all the mixed emotions we experience when we have an enemy and put them toward tasks that would benefit us. I was on top of my game. I was prospecting, closing, and working out. I didn't want to throw myself off track; I had never been so dialed in.

I used the same tactic in November and December of 2021. Ryan posted a Rolex on his story. I'm a watch guy, but I'd never seen this one before. I swiped up to ask what type of watch it was, and he said a Presidential Day Date with a Blue Wave Dial. I looked it up on Google and saw that it cost $60k. I was doing well at that time, but not that well—for a watch, at least.

You may buy a car that costs 25-50% of your annual income, but people usually have a watch that's much less than 10% of their income, and I wasn't making $600k at that time.

I kept scrolling and found a Datejust Jubilee with a blue face for $14k and decided I wanted it, but I was going to follow my rules of money. I wasn't just going to buy it. I would set a huge goal and allow myself to earn it. I told Ryan I was setting a goal for myself, and if I hit it, I would buy it. He told me that if I hit a million in sales in the next 53 days, right before Christmas, he'd buy it for me.

Done.

I was committed.

My biggest month before that was $404k. We'd had an event and expected it to be our biggest month. I didn't know how I would beat that and beat it by another $96k, two months in a row, one after another. But I knew I was committed.

> This is my #1 key
> to hitting goals.
> **Reverse Engineering**.
> Don't stress over a big
> goal; figure out how many
> of each client at each level
> you need to hit it.

I started working the numbers. How many top-level clients did I need at $60k each? How many top-level clients did I feel I could get in in the next two months? What were their names? I needed to write them down and begin cultivating those relationships even more.

Next came second-level clients. With a good majority chunk of that million from Executives, how many Entrepreneurs did I need to pay us $12k? I wrote those peoples' names down, too.

Lastly, low-level. How many people did I need to pay us $2500 to make it happen?

There are two sales lessons in this. First is our Dream 25 concept. This tactic not only got me my first Rolex for free as a gift, but it is responsible for millions of dollars in sales. This one tactic is responsible for nearly half my sales.

Write down the names of 25 of your ideal clients and picture what they look like. Then, start reaching out to them every week and cultivate a relationship. Add them on Facebook, interact with their content, and DM them occasionally. It isn't always sales-y—you just want to stay in front of them and stay top-of-mind. The whole time you should be posting content your ideal client would be interested in, the same way we teach in our Apex program. 80% entertainment, education, personal life; 20% business and client wins. Eventually, they'll reach out, and if you get good at this, every prospect you put on that Dream 25 list will become a client. I have gone through so many of these lists because I sign 90% of the people I write down and focus on.

The next lesson is to focus on the big fish. One Executive client is worth 24 lower clients. If it takes me about the same time to sell a $60k client as it does a $2.5k client, why would I not focus on the $60k client? Especially when they're an easier sell since they know the power of investing in themselves.

By going after the big fish, I lower the number of people I need in my pipeline and how many people I need to follow up with constantly. More often than not, the Executive who can afford to pay $60k to be surrounded by other people paying $60k understands the value of investing a lot more than the entry-level prospect hesitating to invest $2500. The top clients will tell you the same thing—that's probably why they can spend so much with you anyway.

A perfect example: my friend Darian is a roofer and is in our Apex program. He focuses on nothing but high-end residential roofing. These types of houses pay out more than most people do in a month. By focusing on high-end residential clients, he can lessen the number of clients, adjuster meetings, paperwork, contracts signed, etc. On top of that, it's a lot easier for him to double his production—all he has to do is sign up a couple more clients. He definitely doesn't stop after one. I don't know another sales rep in the industry doing the numbers he does.

In Conclusion

"Work like someone is trying to take everything you have away from you."

You hear versions of this saying from some of the greats like Mark Cuban or Dwayne "The Rock" Johnson. Creating an enemy is the same thing, only it allows you to put a face to the person trying to take your goals from you.

Being able to personify that drive, focus, and work ethic will do wonders for you and help make sure you accomplish your goals.

Even if you have to *create* the enemy. Follow me here.

One of the biggest gifts someone can give you is to hate on you or tell you that you can't do something because the minute they do, it will give you a drive like no other.

I remember every time someone doubted me. I use it as fuel for the fire. Don't think of haters as bad; let them fuel you.

Chapter 8

Sean Whalen: What Do You Want?

"The first secret of getting what you want
is knowing what you want."
–Arthur D. Hlavaty

Every year, Apex takes a trip to Cabo San Lucas, Mexico. Most years, we go twice.

We go all-out: charter private jets, take 20 elite entrepreneurs, stay in four mansions in Pedregal, hire private chefs, and have top-notch speakers. The purpose of these trips is not only to show these elite entrepreneurs what FU money is like and the life that is possible if they keep thinking big and growing but also to network, build connections, and learn how to solve the problems standing in the way of owning those jets and mansions. It's an unreal experience, and I highly recommend you make it to one. To learn more, visit ZachSasser1.PhoneSites.com.

Sean Whalen was a guest speaker on one of our trips. We were having dinner when my friend Lee asked Sean how to hit the next level or level up. Sean's response was, "What does that even mean?"

Everyone at the table was kind of taken aback by the answer, but it didn't take long to see what he meant.

He started talking about how 90% of the world is overweight, living paycheck to paycheck, working a 9-5, and Lee obviously wasn't in that group. *So, what did he mean by the next level? What did that next level look like to him? He obviously isn't average.* He paid $15k to be in Cabo with all these elite entrepreneurs and is an elite entrepreneur in his own right, as he's one of the biggest legal, drop shipping drug dealers for veterans in Canada. (I gave him that title, and I love it.)

Furthermore, Sean asked, who did he have to become to hit that next level? Because that's something too many people don't realize; you have to become the person worthy of the results before you get the results.

People like Sean don't get to the position they're in by luck. I knew he was onto something.

Boom.

A light bulb went off.

> What do you want?
> Write it down.

At that time, I was feeling stuck, like God intended for me to do more than what I was doing at the moment, and that was it. I realized I wanted to hit that next level, and that next level for me was helping my brother build an 8-figure roofing company. And I knew exactly how to do it.

I'd been killing it in sales and had hit top producer for the fourth month in a row with Ryan. Complacency is the killer of greatness more often than some terrible catastrophe.

Good is always the killer of great.

It's a lot harder to go after your dreams when you have a comfortable job than if you were at the bottom, and that's exactly where I was: comfortable. It would have been stupid not to use my mentorship under Ryan and our Apex members to build my own companies. I had all the resources, guidance, and mentors I needed; Sean made me realize that fear was the only thing holding me back.

I spent the rest of the night by myself thinking about what that most elite version of myself would look like. To learn what I want. I asked myself: *what do I want?* But not materially, *what do I truly want in life? What did I feel God wanted me to do at that moment?*

I was in beautiful Cabo, Mexico, with Stewman, Sean, and 20 other 8- and 9-figure business owners, and I chose to keep to myself for the rest of the night. Being able to spend that time with yourself and genuinely think and talk to yourself are keys to success. There was nothing anyone else could've told me that night that would've been more powerful than spending the next few hours charting out what I wanted and listening to myself figure out the best plan to get there.

I had to get quiet and focus.

So many people look for people like Sean or other coaches to give them the key to success, but the truth is, Sean helped me pull something out of myself. He didn't give me the game plan; he helped me realize I already knew what I needed—to listen to myself so I could hear it. That's what the best coaches do. They ask questions to help you answer them yourself.

> Get comfortable with more.

I knew I needed to get uncomfortable. I needed to have my back against a wall.

> Simple does not equal easy. A lot of things are simple, but they're not easy."

I started 75 Hard, a "Transformative mental toughness program," after returning from that trip and went to town. (If you haven't done 75 Hard yet, go to 75Hard.com and do it.) Within three days, I knew exactly what I needed to do to take my brother's roofing company to eight figures within the next year. I also started to see a bigger vision.

I saw this book.

I saw what the next chapter in my life looked like as I had just completed one of my most successful ones up to that point by becoming the top producer for a multi-million-dollar consulting business at only 21.

I was on cloud nine and needed to take the bus ride back to Hell.

This was another huge lesson I had to learn. I learned it in my all-time favorite books: *Winning* and *Relentless* by Tim Grover.

Tim Grover is Michael Jordan, Kobe Bryant, and Dwayne Wade's trainer. The dude deals with the Cleaners. If you read *Relentless*, you'll understand what I mean by that, but so that this story makes sense, a Cleaner is a person who wins relentlessly—not at an elite level, but at a legendary level. They are the Tiger Woods, the Tom Bradys, and the Michael Jordans. That level. The next level. He doesn't even include LeBron in the Cleaner league. Read the book, and you'll find out why it makes complete sense.

One of the best lessons anyone has taught me is taking the bus ride back to Hell. When you have that hunger for success, which I'm sure you do if you're reading this book, you're going to become successful. You're going to crush it in life, and it's going to be easy to chase that feeling.

But what people don't think about is that when you chase that high for too long, you won't get to feel that feeling again because you've stopped doing what was required for you to taste that level of success.

You have to take that bus ride back to Hell after winning,
so you can go through the boring, consistent,
and required actions to keep you at that same level
or even take you to the next level.

Maybe you've never won a Super Bowl or a Finals Championship, but chances are you have won in life. You've made a big sale, gotten a good grade on a huge project, made a lot of money, etc. That win gives you a high that doesn't compare to any drug out there. It's addicting. Winning is more fun than fun is fun, but it also makes you want to enjoy the win.

Go out and celebrate, kick your feet up, and feel accomplished. But if you want to consistently win at a high level and be considered among the greats, it is critical that you celebrate the win, then get back to work and take that bus ride back to hell.

Win a Super Bowl on Sunday and be back in the gym that following Monday.

Make a huge sale and get back to prospecting for your next one.

Make a ton of money and invest it so you can't spend it.

Those are all examples of taking that bus ride back to Hell.

If you don't take anything else out of this book, I hope this concept clicks with you because you will NEVER truly become the greatest version of yourself if, along the way, you get too comfortable and allow yourself to enjoy the win too much.

It is crucial that you go back to doing the tedious work required. And I hope this doesn't sound like I don't enjoy my successes and my wins, because I do, but if you're going to truly become elite, you must have that dark side in you where you get back to work immediately. I've learned that as exciting and fulfilling as winning is, it's just as boring because that high doesn't last forever. If you don't take that bus ride back to hell, you won't be winning for long. And I want you to win forever.

But back to what you want.

I know most of my readers are younger, so it's okay if you don't know exactly what that looks like. I still don't know where I will be in 10-20 years. I tell Ryan we'll be in the White House, but that's partly a joke. Pretty profound but partly a joke.

It helps that I don't think too far down the road. I'm a big thinker, so when I say White House, it's really not too far-fetched for that to happen 10-20 years down the road. The possibilities are endless, but to be in a position like that in 10-20 years, I focus on who I need and want to become in the next one, three, and five years.

What do I look like physically?

What do I do on a day-to-day basis?

What type of impact do I have on people?

How do people feel when I'm around them?

How much money do I make?

What type of thoughts do I have?

What type of clothes do I wear?

Where do I live, and with whom?

**Once I know where I want to be,
I reverse-engineer what it will take to get there.**

What do I need to do in the gym and in my diet to look like what I want to look like?

What do I need to do day-to-day now to live the day-to-day I want to then?

How do I need to treat people now so I have an impact on them then?

What do I need to do now to impact how people feel then?

What do I need to do today to make the money I want to make then, etc.?

I could be wrong in saying I don't know where I want to be in 10-20 years. Maybe you are supposed to know because if you don't have a destination plugged into your GPS, you will never get to where you need to be. I know if you don't have a destination, you'll wander around. That's a lot of pressure for someone our age. I'd rather have a general idea so that I'm prepared for the opportunity once I do know. Once again, I don't have all the answers; this is just what has worked for me thus far and what intelligent people around me have helped me with.

I know I want to have multiple businesses, investments, rental properties, passive investment streams, a family around me that loves me and knows I'll do anything for them, be in great shape, and be able to work through whatever adversity life throws at me because I have a tough and sharp mindset, etc. I guess that when God wants me to know my next chapter, he will start revealing clues. Until then, my goal is to crush my current chapter and position myself where I need to be to crush my next chapter!

Chapter 9

Big Brother Leads the Way

"Learn from the mistakes of others.
You can't live long enough to make them all yourself."
—Eleanor Roosevelt

Have you ever played a racing game and switched the camera angle? You can play the game with the angle up high where you can see the back of the car and the front, or you can play it with the camera angle inside the car looking through the windshield as if you were actually sitting in the car.

That's how I view my brother's and my perspectives. He was the firstborn and had to figure things out from that first-person perspective, and I always got to sit back and watch him with a wider view.

Growing up, Brett always experienced things first, and I would always tag along with him and observe. I learned quickly that when you hang out with older boys, you need to stay quiet and not try to be the center of attention. The less you say, the less chance you have of saying something wrong. If I just sat back, observed, and played it cool, they'd let me hang out with them. That made me a very observant person and has led to a lot of my success in sales.

Every time I'm in that first-person view, I feel like I make more mistakes and can't see or think clearly—but when I'm in that back position, I can

> Make things as simple as possible. Don't make business complicated. Have a great product—an irresistible offer. An offer so good, they would be dumb to say no.

see the whole screen and maneuver how I need to. I can make the right decisions, solve problems, and think clearly. When someone else is the main character, I can think without clouded judgment.

I don't know if it's an anxiety or stress thing, whether I put too much pressure on myself or think too hard, but for whatever reason, I am almost always better in that widescreen mode, that player two position, letting someone else drive the car while I direct and navigate from up top. Whether it's in life with my older brother, in business with my older brother, with Stewman, or whatever I'm doing, I'm much better helping from the background than being the main guy.

Just recently, Stewman interviewed Fat Joe, and Fat Joe talked about how you need to know when you are #1 and know when you are #2. In Joe's life, no matter how successful he becomes, when he gets around his brother, he always falls in as that #2.

I use that metaphor to tell that story because it comes down to knowing yourself. This is a huge lesson that not enough people focus on. At the end of the day, I can give you all the advice in the world, but all that advice is what I've learned works best for me and most of the people I'm around. If something doesn't feel right to you, maybe it's not how you operate. It really comes down to finding how you operate best and becoming the most efficient in that area.

Someone could tell me to hit the phones for eight hours a day, and I could. Or I could strategically set up my day to get on the phone for a couple of hours and set up breaks every 20-30 minutes because I know I'm not efficient after 20-30 minutes of intense focus.

Someone could tell me to wake up at 5 a.m., but if I know I'm most creative, active, and have my best thoughts at night, I'd be a fool to go to bed at 9 p.m. when I could stay up until 11 or 12 and knock out work like I am now, writing this at 10 at night. So, I wake up a little later and get the amount of sleep I need since I need to be in peak mindset and give my body enough time to heal from working out and building my muscles.

Someone could tell me how they feel I should act as a sales rep, but if I want to be better than everyone else, then I can't do the same stuff they do.

I know I am better in that player two position and steering the boat, but I like having a captain whom I can help maneuver the ship even better. I don't want to be the only one to do it.

Another example: someone may tell you your network is important and you should go out to meet people, but if you know you're an introvert, maybe there's a better way to meet people.

Believe it or not, Stewman and I are both introverts. We'll go meet people, but we can't wait to get away from the party. That's knowing yourself.

I am very intentional in how I go into social settings and set myself up exactly how I need to meet the people I need to so I can make the sales I need, and dip from there.

Nobody could've taught me that in a book; it just comes down to knowing myself, self-analyzing, and thinking logically to find my best plan of action. I know I can pop out of a social setting for 10-15 minutes and come back recharged to put myself in a much better position, but I didn't learn that from anyone. That's learning and listening to yourself.

The ability to self-reflect and truly be honest with yourself are some of the most valuable skills you can have.

Realize where you're lacking. My competitiveness recently started taking over, and I could tell. It was affecting my thoughts and more areas of my life. So I talked to a couple of our Apex Executives, and they talked me through it. They said it was good I felt that way because that's what makes us great, but it was also great that I could self-reflect and realize when it was crossing the line.

Analyze how you're living your life versus your end goal of how you want your life to be. Nobody is babysitting you. It is up to you to accomplish all your dreams, and that starts with being able to analyze yourself, your actions, your thoughts, your motives, your skills, your advantages, and disadvantages—everything.

Chances are that whatever way someone has of doing something right now can be improved anyway. Instead of just trusting everyone to have the absolute best system, try thinking for yourself and outside the box. Find a better solution.

Trust yourself.

Listen to yourself.

Learn to self-reflect and self-analyze.

As much as I recommend having a mentor and learning from the experiences and wisdom of others, sometimes all you need to do is listen to what you already know and get in touch with yourself.

Chapter 10

Jose: Thinking Big

"Most people overestimate what they can accomplish in a year—
and underestimate what they can achieve in a decade!"
—Tony Robbins

Just about every day, my dude Jose and I eat lunch together. We've gotten better at meal prepping and bringing our lunch, but it was literally every day for a while. It probably wasn't the healthiest choice, but I was more focused on other aspects of my life then, so diet wasn't a big deal. I concentrated more on the conversations Jose and I would have.

For those who don't know Jose, he's one of the smartest dudes I know. From running the cartels to running marketing budgets for multi-million-dollar companies, the dude is also one of the most interesting people I know. Every day at lunch, I'd learn something new from him. I mentioned earlier how I learned about enemies from him and how to fight and think big.

> You are who you
> surround yourself with.
> They think big.
> You'll think big.
> They get jacked.
> You'll get jacked.
> They have good relationships.
> You'll have good relationships.

One day, we went to an Italian restaurant. Our conversation was different than usual. It was just after someone I had looked up to had become one of my biggest haters, so Jose talked me through that.

He started prophesying to me that I was meant for big things. That what I'm focused on right now is just the beginning. Where this hater, a grown man, was right now was where I was at 21, but in ten years, he would be in the same spot, and I'd be way ahead. It all comes down to where you think you'll be.

If you set your goal at $100k, you'll probably find a way to make $100k and won't go too far past that. But if your goal is $100M, hitting it might take you longer, but you'll probably find your way to that goal you set for yourself. Your only limitation is how big you think.

> Find the balance between comparing yourself to those way ahead of you and knowing they were nowhere near where you are when they were your age. It'll happen. Trust the process and enjoy the journey.

I realized that you will accomplish what you think you can. This was a crazy epiphany to me.

> Keep your goals huge. Keep growing, but take time for yourself. You are your biggest asset.

Growing up, "six-figure income" is the benchmark for many. While you go through school, everyone talks about how they want to make six figures. But who decided that needed to be the standard? Why can't it be more?

We are constantly getting ceilings placed on us. The world, the school system, and the government operate in a way meant for average people because they have to.

I don't mean that in a narcissistic, "I think I'm better" way; I just mean that statistically speaking, there will be a distribution curve, and most people will fall in the middle. Some will be lower, and some will be higher. But you must understand that society is geared toward those people in the middle.

> The goal is to become the best person in the room, then find a new room.

They're happy with the 9-5, corporate rat race, the safe paycheck. They're fine growing up, having some kids, the white picket fence, etc. And there's absolutely nothing wrong with that if that's what you want. But if you do want to go on and do great things, if you do want to influence millions of people, change the world, grow things that the average human couldn't dream of, and so on, then you can't think the same way that our society and world is programming you to think.

You have to think bigger!

I have always heard that cliché that you are who you hang out with. It was just a common phrase until I was surrounded by a network of people who truly challenged me and made me look in the mirror and analyze where I was and where I wanted to be. They made me get serious about accomplishing my goals. I'm a huge believer in that for multiple reasons that I'll discuss in the next chapter. The people around you teach you, support you, share ideas; they set your temperature on what's possible.

Ed Mylett talks about this often. He calls it your internal thermostat. Think of how a thermostat works. If it is set to 70 degrees, but the door is open, the room may get hot. Even if you leave the door open, that thermostat will eventually bring the temperature back to 70. It may get cold too, but the thermostat at 70 will eventually bring the temperature back up to 70.

You have a figurative thermostat in every aspect of your life.

If your financial thermostat is set to $100k, you'll eventually find your way to it, and no matter how bad things get or how good things get, you'll find a way to make extra money to get back to $100k, or you'll find a way to spend extra money to get back down to 100k. That's because of where your thermostat is set.

Physically, maybe 180 lbs. is where you look and feel best. You may lose or gain some weight, but you'll eventually find your way back to 180. It's your normal. It's where your thermostat is set.

Jose told me that I'm around many very successful people in our Apex program, which has raised my temperature, but I had gotten to a point where I was comfortable. I thought my level of sales was good. I thought my body looked good. I was JUST COMFORTABLE. But you have to think bigger. There are literal billionaires out there who are no more special than you. They just think like billionaires. That's where their thermostats are set.

If we aren't thinking big, then what are we doing?

Chapter 11

Fraternity: Enjoying Life

"Life is too short to be doing the things you don't love doing."
—Bruce Dickinson

I'm 22. I graduated high school in May of 2018.

I told y'all that growing up, I wanted to go to Stanford and become an engineer. When I decided engineering wasn't my calling, I started to doubt going to college.

It's become popular to say you don't need a college degree to be a business owner or entrepreneur, and I agree that it isn't necessary. But I had knocked out almost my entire first year of college by "double dipping" high school and AP credits. Also, I got a scholarship to pay for half of my school, so I decided it wouldn't hurt. I would stay focused on my education (in the real world) while I mastered using Microsoft Excel in college.

The truth is you don't need college to be successful. It isn't binary. People make it seem as if those that don't go to college won't be successful. The truth is I know plenty of very successful people that went and plenty of successful people that didn't.

If you are thinking about going, go. If you don't want to, don't. I had fun, met some lifelong friends, learned a ton about myself, and it helped in my transition into life. I am glad I went, but it's not because of the knowledge or the degree. It was because it was what I made of it. So that is the best advice I can give you on formal education versus informal education. Just choose one way or another, don't stress like I did.

I'm going to get vulnerable with y'all because I feel that's the only way to be. In my first year of college, I became depressed. I had never experienced depression before, but suddenly I had no friends nearby. All my high school friends moved far away while I went to North Texas, ten minutes from where I grew up, and because I lived at home, I didn't have any dorm friends.

I would go to class, to the gym and then go home. My life had changed so much from being popular in high school, having all my football buddies, and knowing everyone. It messed me up for a while. Sometimes new chapters do that to you. I didn't want that to be my college experience.

In high school, I was very focused. I was huge on staying in on the weekends to work and study and knew it would get me ahead. I'm also introverted, so it was rare that I wanted to hang out with too many people.

But one of my high school friends joined a sorority, and her cousin was in a fraternity. He'd been trying to get me to join since my senior year in high school, but I didn't see myself as a "frat boy."

But when I realized that all the guys in the fraternity reminded me of my high school friends, I decided I wanted to check it out. Worst case: *I don't like it and don't join.* Best case: *I meet some of my best friends, have exposure to great business networking opportunities, and enjoy college.*

It ended up being the latter.

I enjoyed college, let loose a little (which isn't the easiest for me to do), and I truly grew into a man during the years I was in Sigma Chi. I found a group of guys to do life with. Since then, three of my fraternity brothers now work at Apex with me, two are at Lonestar Exterior, and I am sure I will employ hundreds of Sigma Chi's throughout my life.

Fraternity Lesson #1

I told this story because joining Sig taught me not to take life so seriously.

Throughout high school, I stayed focused on work. I don't regret it since I wouldn't have the financial and business success I do now if I hadn't made those sacrifices. But I wish I had lived a little bit more, made more memories, and let loose sometimes.

You may not have realized it, but life is short. I've already felt regret in the short time I've been on this Earth, and it hurt enough to know I never wanted to feel like that again.

Yes, be successful, and handle your business. Outwork everyone. Make sacrifices. Excel in every aspect of your life and crush it, but don't forget to find that balance for yourself. It isn't all about money or growing businesses. Go meet new people, create memories, take risks, and join different groups. Experience life, man.

Don't chase the money.
Chase gratitude.
Chase happiness.
Chase the memories and experiences money can buy you.
Chase freedom.

The Bible doesn't say money is the root of all evil; it says the *love* of money is the root of all evil.

Money is important.

Without money, you can't even buy water, and you need water to live.

But do not chase money.

Forget the people who tell you to grind your life away. I truly love the grind, and it's hard to turn my brain off from focusing on growth and opportunities. But I know if I don't find a way to force my brain off and intentionally spend time with those I care about, I'll look up 60 years from now (if I'm lucky) and regret that I was so focused on growing businesses that I didn't meet some of the best people who could've been in my life or created some of the best memories possible.

It's all about finding what that balance is for you. There's a fine line because you must distinguish between having a lack of discipline and being intentional with living.

I see many people who get stuck in the partying lifestyle, become out of control, and allow it to affect their goals and drive. No judgment, but that way of life isn't aligned with my goals and how I want to live. That may be their idea of balance and enjoying their one shot on this planet. It isn't my life. And if you're reading this, you probably don't fall into that category either.

So, be disciplined. Find ways to delay your gratification. Be hard on yourself, but don't forget to live.

Set goals.

Crush them.

Then reward yourself.

Be intentional with how you live your life.

Excel in all areas of your life, including living and letting loose.

Fraternity Lesson #2

Another thing the fraternity taught me was that sales make the world go round in the business world.

This especially applies when you get into scalability and build recurring sales, passive income, and even sales teams under you—the really big opportunities excelling at sales provides. They are the best way to reach that million-dollar mark, but that's not what this section is about.

This section will show you an example of problem-solving and how essential sales is. When you are sales-minded, you can solve many issues. In 2020, COVID-19 shut down our world while my fraternity went through tough financial times. Long story short, the brothers who came before us didn't know how money worked, nor did they pay their financial dues, so they left a significant weight for us to carry.

Many people focus on having jobs to make salaries. You can search online for jobs with the biggest salaries while trying to figure out what you want to do with your life, but without sales and marketing, companies can't pay their employees' salaries.

Salespeople have the most valuable and safest job, but definitely not the easiest. Once you go through the fire and come out the other side a sales boss, you become bulletproof in the job force sense. You have no income cap; your skills will always be sought (if you decide not to work for yourself) and you can fast-forward your journey toward financial freedom.

When you make money for a company money instead of costing it money, you become their biggest asset.

Luckily for them, I was their #3 man in charge, and I've had some of the best marketing and sales training and mentors out there. So, I approached the problem with a "how can we make money from this?" mindset.

Then, I started looking for ways to make money. We already sold shirts, but at cost and there was no profit. I'm not sure who came up with the idea not to profit from those sales, but selling shirts for profit presented an ideal way to raise money.

I started thinking about how to increase the number of shirts we sold, the profit from each sale, and what new shirt styles could offer.

Who would want to buy a shirt from us? Alumni, sorority girls, parents of brothers, and even the general public. I found a way to create a business within our fraternity and put all the profit toward getting us out of our financial hole.

**It's crazy to me how much sales
can impact every area of your life.**

I'm not selling you on learning sales. Do you. Follow your heart. But I would highly recommend checking it out. It changed my life.

Overall, it's easy to get into the grind and hustle and work your tail end off, and I highly recommend doing so. Life is a whole lot better when you're willing to put in the work, make sacrifices, and delay your gratification. You do what others won't early on so you can do what others can't later on: live off passive investments, take your family on unlimited vacations (or, better yet, just live where you'd want to vacation), and not have to miss your kids' soccer games. But don't get so caught up in the grind that you forget to live.

"The Station" by Robert Hastings

Tucked away in our subconscious minds is an idyllic vision. We see ourselves on a long, long trip that almost spans the continent. We're traveling by passenger train, and out the windows we drink in the passing scene of cars on nearby highways, of children waving at a crossing, of cattle grazing on a distant hillside, of smoke pouring from a power plant, of row upon row of corn and wheat, of flatlands and valleys, of mountains and rolling hills, of biting winter and blazing summer and cavorting spring and docile fall.

But uppermost in our minds is the final destination. On a certain day at a certain hour we will pull into the station. There will be bands playing, and flags waving. And once we get there so many wonderful dreams will come true. So many wishes will be fulfilled and so many pieces of our lives finally will be neatly fitted together like a completed jigsaw puzzle. How restlessly we pace the aisles, damning the minutes for loitering ... waiting, waiting, waiting, for the station.

However, sooner or later we must realize there is no one station, no one place to arrive at once and for all. The true joy of life is the trip. The station is only a dream. It constantly outdistances us.

"When we reach the station, that will be it!" we cry. Translated it means, "When I'm 18, that will be it! When I buy a new 450 SL Mercedes Benz, that will be it! When I put the last kid through college, that will be it! When I have paid off the mortgage, that will be it! When I win a promotion, that will be it! When I reach the age of retirement, that will be it! I shall live happily ever after!"

Unfortunately, once we get it, then it disappears. The station somehow hides itself at the end of an endless track.

"Relish the moment" is a good motto, especially when coupled with Psalm 118:24: "This is the day which the Lord hath made; we will rejoice and be glad in it." It isn't the burdens of today that drive men mad. Rather, it is regret over yesterday or fear of tomorrow. Regret and fear are twin thieves who would rob us of today.

So, stop pacing the aisles and counting the miles. Instead, climb more mountains, eat more ice cream, go barefoot oftener, swim more rivers, watch more sunsets, laugh more and cry less. Life must be lived as we go along. The station will come soon enough.

People feel like they'll be happy after they get that car, put their kid through college, etc. But they don't realize the journey is the true gift.

There is no destination.

You're not going to magically be happy or satisfied once you reach your end goal; it's all in the journey.

That's the best way I can summarize this chapter: live your life, have goals, and work hard, but remember there is no train station.

There is no end destination.

Enjoy the ride.

So many times, we find ourselves wandering. Napoleon Hill talks about this in his book, *Outwitting the Devil*. "Drifting," as he calls it, is the Devil's number one tool in adopting people to the dark side and not knowing where you want to go or why, not taking actionable steps to get there, etc. Knowing where you want to go and where you are right now is important. "Take Inventory" is what I call it.

Here is an exercise I use to figure out where I am, what I'm comfortable with, and what stepping out of that comfort zone would look like, as it is crucial to growth. Take a few minutes and outline your inventory.

Take Inventory Exercise

Write down where you are and everything you're comfortable with—making $6k a month, waking up at 7 a.m., working out three times per week, spending $4k a month and saving $2k a month, dating girls for a few weeks before breaking up with them.

Then, list the things that make you uncomfortable—staying in a committed relationship, working out every day, waking up at 6 a.m., eating 3500 calories a day, making $10k a month and saving $5k a month, and so on.

Now, commit to making changes that make you uncomfortable. Start with one thing, make it a habit, then move on to the next.

Repeat this exercise every few months. Once you start making more money, raise your comfort level.

Once you hit your income goal, raise it.

Once you start waking up earlier, push it a bit more.

Save more.

Invest more.

Keep searching for the right significant other.

You should constantly be improving.

You should constantly be making progress.

You don't have to be the richest, strongest, wisest, etc.

You just need to make progress.

Chapter 12

Defining Winning

"The fellow whose verdict counts most in your
life is the one staring back from the glass."
—From the poem "The Man in the Glass" by Peter Dale Wimbrow Sr.

What is winning?

People have varying definitions of winning; to some, it looks like having nice cars and spending money on nice things. I love cars and nice things, but because I'm at a different place in my life and have different perspectives, win-

> Focus on 2 things:
> Things that make you money and things that you enjoy doing.

ning to me looks like working hard while I'm young and investing my money so that my investments pay for those nice things in 5-10 years.

To some, winning looks like winning an argument; to me, winning looks like putting my ego aside to put myself in the best position possible.

For instance, it's okay to let others think they won when it comes to drama at work. Go back to your definition of winning, and don't look at anyone else. Others can win alongside you; there's enough for everyone. Don't let your ego and winning a battle cause you to lose a war.

Don't let an argument with your spouse ruin something special. Put your ego to the side and go back to your definition of winning.

> I'm working now so I can buy back my time.

Is winning making money? Or is it making money without sacrificing your health, mental, relationships, and social life?

Ultimately, you have to get into the mindset that it doesn't matter what others do, think, or define as successful. *What does it look like to me?*

Selling a business for $100M? Owning a fraction of a company that sells for $100M? Having your bills covered by passive investments with no stress? Changing lives?

People are at different places in their lives. My definition of winning today will be different from my definition ten years from now. It has to be something you know in your heart, not what other people think winning looks like for you.

What do YOU want? I mean, REALLY want?

"The Man in The Glass" by Peter Dale Wimbrow, Sr.

When you get what you want in your struggle for self

And the world makes you king for a day

Just go to the mirror and look at yourself

And see what that man has to say.

For it isn't your father, or mother, or wife

Whose judgment upon you must pass

The fellow whose verdict counts most in your life

Is the one staring back from the glass.

He's the fellow to please—never mind all the rest

For he's with you, clear to the end

And you've passed your most difficult, dangerous test

If the man in the glass is your friend.

You may fool the whole world down the pathway of years

And get pats on the back as you pass

But your final reward will be heartache and tears

If you've cheated the man in the glass.

In Closing

You made it to the end; you're already separating yourself from the pack by finishing a book.

But the work isn't done.

I wrote this book to give you the edge to get even closer to becoming the greatest version of yourself. To help you get even closer to being in that top 1% of the 1%, not only financially but in every aspect of your life. To help you be more ambitious and realize you aren't the only one out there to come across these problems, and to help give you some of the best advice and information I have been blessed with by having so many knowledgeable mentors.

As you wrap up this book, remember that the world will throw every distraction at you.

A friend discouraging you from your crazy business idea.

Impostor syndrome keeping you from feeling as if you can accomplish your goals.

Whatever it is, you cannot let that affect your long-term vision and goals.

Life will always be challenging. It's a roller coaster. Some days you will feel you can accomplish anything you set your mind to, and on others, you will feel like giving up.

Prioritize your long-term goals over any short-term feelings.

Too many people believe in you and want you to succeed for you to give up, whether you know who those people are yet or not.

I try my best not to be philosophical, but life is a journey.

As you go on this journey, you will meet people, and those people will lead you to meet more people. You're going to learn, and you're going to get better and better.

You'll go through pain.

You'll find joy.

You'll have highs.

And you'll have lows.

But the further you go, the wiser you will get and the more understanding you'll have.

You'll meet mentors like the ones I've mentioned in this book. If you're lucky, you'll meet all of them and learn the same lessons they taught me. But do yourself and them a favor, and don't take it for granted.

Growing up poor was a disadvantage until I realized it was an advantage.

Working hard was hard until my dad taught me it was non-negotiable.

Life was complicated until Stewman taught me there are four areas of life to win in.

Entrepreneurship was complicated until Dan showed me it could be simple.

I let my enemies affect me until Jose taught me to make them fuel for me.

I was overwhelmed until Sean told me to get clear on what I wanted.

I felt like a failure and outcast until my brother showed me I could be my own person.

I thought my dreams were too big until Jose told me that was how it should be.

I thought life was all about accomplishing goals until Sigma Chi taught me to have fun with it because you won't make it out alive.

And I was chasing something I didn't even want until our Apex Executives helped me realize what I really wanted in life.

I can't give these mentors enough credit. People look at me as the golden boy, but I wouldn't be where I am without every lesson they've taught me along this journey.

Everything they've poured into me has gotten me to this point. And I only plan on learning more, working harder, and helping more people.

I'm not entirely sure where that will take me. I love building businesses, making sales, investing my money, and helping others do the same.

My plans are broken down into simple goals, but life happens while you're making plans. All you can control is what you do today, so I'm focused on winning today, getting one step closer to that greatest version of myself, and enjoying the process.

Thank you for reading my book. If it gave you just one piece of advice, one actionable item, one sentence that challenged the way you think about or live your life, then the months and months it took me to write it were worth it.

Throughout my life, I have taken the information and knowledge that people have poured into me and created a good foundation for building an empire. I want you to do the same. Information is pointless if you don't do anything with it. You've got millions of dollars' worth of game. Now it's time to find what works for you, make things as simple as possible, and get dialed into hitting whatever success is for you.

If you liked what I had to say, please feel free to connect with me at:

ZachSasser.com

Facebook.com/RealZachSasser

Instagram @Sasser21.

I'm also including a list of the books and programs that have had the most significant impact on me and helped to get me to where I am.

My Top Books Are

- *Relentless* by Tim Grover

- *Winning* by Tim Grover

- *GCode* by Ryan Stewman

- *Elevator to the Top* by Ryan Stewman

- *The Perfect Day to Boss Up* Rick Ross

- *75 Hard* by Andy Frisella

- *Think and Grow Rich* by Napoleon Hill

- *The Way of the Superior Man* by David Deida

- *Whale Done!* by Ken Blanchard

- *The 21 Irrefutable Laws of Leadership* by John C. Maxwell

- *The 48 Laws of Power* By Robert Greene

- *The Ultimate Sales Machine* by Chet Holmes

- *The Greatest Salesman in the World* by Og Mandino

- *Extreme Ownership* by Jocko Willink and Leif Babin

Acknowledgments

I once heard, "There is no such thing as self-made." As much as that term is thrown out there, I agree. Ultimately, it is up to you to dream, do the work, stay committed, etc. But it most definitely is a team effort to build something special.

I want to thank my family. I'm a huge believer in choosing your family over the family that God gives you. Luckily, I would choose the family God gave me over anything else.

Thank you, Mom, for raising me to be the gentleman I have become, teaching me how to treat a woman, taking care of me, and being my rock in this crazy world.

Thank you, Dad, for being a shining example of a father who leads his family and molding me into the man I needed to be.

Thank you to my brothers, Brett, Kyle, and Ty, for being my built-in best friends. I've always been a bit of a loner, but they have been by my side through everything.

I want to thank Ryan Stewman for giving me an opportunity—an opportunity to be great. I made sure to take advantage of it. Without Ryan, I wouldn't have learned most of these lessons. I wouldn't have written a book; I wouldn't have shortened my success curve drastically. I wouldn't be impacting as many people, but most of all, I wouldn't have been shaped into the leader, young man, hustler, and Young Closer I have become.

I want to thank my friends. Over the years, this term has changed, but I want to thank them all. They are the ones who stuck by my side through everything, the ones who have held me down and kept my head on straight. I thank even the ones I no longer associate with because they made me a stronger man. Who you surround yourself with will determine where you end up, and I am blessed to have a great handful of people I choose to give my time to and to level up with.

Last but not least, I want to thank everybody who has ever interacted with me. It's tough to include the thousands of people who have helped me, especially those who have genuinely helped me. The truth is, there aren't too many people in my life who haven't made me a better person or shaped me into the man I am now. From the bottom of my heart, thank you.

You have no clue how grateful I am and the lessons you instilled in me. Your impact on me will go on and make a ripple effect throughout the world.

About the Author

At age 22, author Zach Sasser has experienced more than most 42-year-olds. Growing up in an entrepreneurial family and being exposed to the business and personal development world inspired Zach to become the greatest version of himself in every aspect of life.

Being surrounded by the best mentors in the game has allowed him to shortcut his success drastically instead of learning the hard way. From childhood lessons to learning about digital marketing and business in high school to having million-dollar conversations on private jets, Zach has compiled quite a track record at a very early age.

He has racked up millions in sales, built multiple companies, has hundreds of thousands in investments, and has a network that could go to bat against just about any 22-year-old. Zach has taken what he has learned and run with it. With experience comes lessons, failure, and wins. While most choose to act like their life is perfect, Zach prefers to be honest about his wins and losses.

His intention in writing this book is to condense the condenser—to simplify what he has learned and help put you, the reader, on a fast path to success—not just in business but in life.

Zach doesn't believe in luck, so he has worked endlessly to get to where he is now. He thinks it would be selfish not to share the lessons he has learned along the way with the world.

Disclaimer

The advice and events outlined in this book are for informational purposes only. The reader relies on said advice and circumstances at his/her own risk. The results of taking any actions outlined in this book may vary, and the author and publisher make no guarantees regarding any results.

Made in the USA
Middletown, DE
18 October 2022

12973808R00066